Medical information: a profile

Medical information: a profile

Barry Strickland-Hodge and Barbara Allan

Knowledge Industry Publications, Inc.
White Plains, New York

First U.S. edition, 1986
Knowledge Industry Publications, Inc., 701 Winchester Ave.,
White Plains, NY

© Barry Strickland-Hodge and Barbara Allan, 1986

All rights reserved. No part of this publication may be reproduced or transmitted, in any form or by any means, electronic or mechanical, including photocopy, recording or any information storage or retrieval system, without permission in writing from the publishers or their appointed agents.

Library of Congress Cataloging-in-Publication Data

Strickland-Hodge, Barry.
   Medical information.

   Includes index.
   1. Medicine—Bibliography. 2. Reference books—Medicine—Bibliography. 3. Medicine—Information services—Bibliography. 4. On-line bibliographic searching. I. Allan, Barbara C. II. Title. [DNLM: 1. Bibliography of Medicine. 2. Information Services—directories. 3. Information Systems. ZWB 100 S917m]
Z6658.S92   1985   [R129]   016.61   85-19726
ISBN 0-86729-1063-X

Printed in Great Britain

Contents

Introduction		vii
1	Printed sources of information in medicine	1
	1.1 Literature guides	1
	1.2 Dictionaries	5
	1.3 Encyclopedias	10
	1.4 Directories	11
	1.5 Handbooks and databooks	16
	1.6 Patents	20
	1.7 Report literature	25
	1.8 Bibliographies	26
	1.9 Periodicals	29
	1.10 Abstracting and indexing journals	35
	1.11 Theses	45
	1.12 Research in progress	47
2	Online information retrieval	49
	2.1 Online information systems	49
	2.2 Computer hardware	53
	2.3 Computer software	55
	2.4 Searching online	55
	2.5 Future developments	59
	2.6 Further information	59
	2.7 Individual databases	60
	2.8 Videotex	67
3	Organizations and people	77
	3.1 International organizations	78
	3.2 The health services	79
	3.3 Professional groups	80
	3.4 The library service	80
	3.5 Drug information units	82
	3.6 Government bodies	82
	3.7 Professional associations	84
	3.8 Academic institutions	86
	3.9 Research institutes	87
	3.10 Commercial organizations	87

	3.11 Voluntary organizations	88
	3.12 Individuals	89

4 Search strategy — 91

    4.1 Basic requirements — 91
    4.2 Getting to grips with the topic — 91
    4.3 Abstracting and indexing journals — 93
    4.4 Bringing the search up to date — 94
    4.5 Other sources useful in searching — 94
    4.6 Online searching techniques — 95

5 Case studies — 105

    5.1 Sources used by general practitioners — 105
    5.2 Searching for drug information — 106
    5.3 Case studies — 108
    5.4 Searching a multidisciplinary subject: toxicology — 120

6 Organizing medical information — 127

    6.1 Information records — 127
    6.2 Contents of information records — 128
    6.3 Subject access to information — 130
    6.4 Use of microcomputers to organize information — 132

Index — 139

Introduction

The purpose of this book is to assist those involved or intending to become involved in searching medical information. Many people currently use medical information sources; for example: medical, dental and nursing students; medical practitioners in hospital and general practice; research workers in university or polytechnics, hospitals and within the pharmaceutical industry; pharmacists in hospitals, private practice and industry; and patients at home or in hospital.

The information needs of these various groups are very different, and even within a particular group there will be an enormous range of needs. A research worker involved on a project concerned with AIDS and located in a hospital will have quite different needs from someone carrying out research on the development of a new pharmaceutical product for a drug company. It would be an impossible task to try to write a book that would satisfy the information needs of all medical information searchers. It is, however, possible to give some general guidelines on information searching, and to show how a variety of problems may be approached.

The book is *not* an exhaustive bibliography; it is a selective collection of sources of medical information covering the major *types* of source such as literature guides and abstracting journals. It also gives specific details of individual examples such as *MIMS* and *Index Medicus*. The sources chosen are those often encountered by searchers, and many of them have associated searching problems. Some sources useful in medicine, such as patents, are often ignored because of their apparent complexity. When a useful but problematic source of this kind has been chosen for inclusion in this book, it is discussed in detail with an explanation of its usefulness and hints as to how it can best be exploited. Straightforward sources are allotted less detailed explanation, though we have attempted to point out the strengths and weaknesses of all the sources we have included. An important aim of this book is to provide a *practical* rather than a theoretical guide to medical information sources.

The structure of the book falls into three parts. The first (Chapter 1) looks at printed sources, the second (Chapters 2–4) considers other sources, organizations and searching techniques. The final part (Chapters 5 and 6) uses case studies to show how searches can be carried out, and discusses techniques for organizing the information retrieved during the searches.

Chapter 1 is a detailed consideration of each of the selective list of printed sources of information in medicine. The first type of source considered is literature guides which, as their name suggests, are guides to finding information on a particular topic, such as nursing, or to a particular type of information, such as statistical sources. They are of use to someone just beginning to search in a new topic for the first time.

Secondly, we look at dictionaries. Of course everyone is familiar with using a dictionary but possibly less well known are the wide range of dictionaries which are available in the field of medicine and the advantages and disadvantages of particular dictionaries. This section is followed by a brief look at encyclopedias, which though of great importance in general information searches are of little value to medical information seekers.

The next section is concerned with directories, which are publications that provide lists of names and addresses or other useful items of information. As there are currently thousands of directories in print, we start by looking at how to find out about them. We move on to list some useful directories and give tips and hints on how to use them. Like directories, handbooks and databooks contain factual information and can be used to provide answers to specific questions. Rather than try to provide an overview of all medical handbooks and databooks we look at two specific fields, drug information and statistics, and provide an indication of what the important handbooks in these fields are and how best to use them.

Patents are another source of factual information and they are a source which is often forgotten by medical information searchers. Patents are important, as they contain detailed technical information which may not be available elsewhere or may not be otherwise available until a later date. As information searchers may not be familiar with the patent literature this section starts by describing the information tools that are provided by patent offices. Printed abstracting and indexing journals which are either wholly devoted to the patent literature or cover patents relevant to a particular subject field are then described, and online patent information sources are touched on.

The next section covers the report literature. Information available in reports is often fuller and more detailed than in the papers that may follow. They are available from government, industry and academic institutions and should not be forgotten when searching.

Bibliographies, which are lists of books or other information sources, are important aids to searching and are described and discussed under the headings general bibliographies, general medical bibliographies and specialized bibliographies. This section concludes with guidance on finding out about new books and describes some important information sources in this area.

The preceding types of information source, with the possible exception of patents, are all out of date by the time they are published. Medical workers require up-to-date information and must turn to the periodical literature, which is the normal mode of publishing the results of research. Although individual periodicals are not discussed in detail, much space is given to describing how to trace them. One important means of enabling the information worker to cope with the massive journal literature is the abstracting or indexing journal. Major examples such as *Index Medicus* and *Excerpta Medica* are described in detail.

Searching printed abstracting and indexing journals is tedious and time-consuming. Online searching (that is, searching computerized databases) overcomes these problems and also enables more detailed searches to be carried out. The next chapter begins with a very basic, non-technical description of the hardware and the software needed to carry out an online search. It continues with a detailed description of how to carry out the search itself, including suggestions of what to do if things go wrong! The chapter looks at individual online databases and then moves on to another type of computerized information source—videotex. The two available forms of videotex, teletext and viewdata, are described with reference to the types of medical information which they contain.

Chapter 3 moves from printed or computerized information sources to an extremely important source of information which is frequently overlooked—organizations and people. As individuals with expert knowledge are normally associated with an organization, the two are considered together. A wide range of organizations, for example drug information units, commercial organizations and voluntary organizations, are considered together with information on how to trace a suitable organization for a particular purpose, if one exists. The chapter concludes with a guide to finding out about individuals.

Chapter 4 considers in detail the process of carrying out an information search, and thus draws together the various resources described in the earlier chapters and shows how they can be combined in as wide a search as is necessary for the particular application. The decisions that must be made at each stage of the search are indicated.

The final part of the book looks first at the specific information needs of groups of people, taking as examples general practitioners and retail pharmacists. It then deals with specific searches in topics such as sickle cell anaemia and within complex subject areas such as toxicology. Case studies of actual searches are included to show how and when each source can be used and what information can be expected from it. The final section of the book looks at methods of organizing medical information whatever its type, by means of both manual and computerized systems.

It is envisaged that this book will be of use to medical librarians, general practitioners who wish to carry out a search, pharmacists, researchers, nurses and any other interested individual within the health care teams. To summarize, it looks at a selected range of sources from the viewpoint of their usefulness in medicine and gives some consideration to searching through each source. The more complex the source the more space is given to its discussion. Because the book is necessarily selective, some types of source, such as audiovisual materials, government publications and atlases, have largely been ignored. This book is a guide, a search tool, and we hope an invaluable aid to searching medical information.

1 Printed sources of information in medicine

1.1 Literature guides

A literature guide aims to assist the user with the information sources on a particular topic. Guides to the literature are prime tools for anyone trying to seek out information, and they are particularly useful when searching in an unfamiliar subject field or a particular type of literature; for example, government publications. Every subject has its own particular structure and a literature with its own special characteristics, and a guide is a useful short cut to utilizing the literature on that subject effectively. Similarly, different types of information source—for example, government publications, audiovisual materials, computerized databases—all have their own peculiar means of bibliographic control, distribution and development and it is important to be aware of them if these information sources are to be used effectively.

Thus when carrying out any information search, it is a worthwhile first step to check whether there is a literature guide on the chosen subject. If there is, it can then be used to provide a list of relevant information sources, to obtain tips on carrying out an information search, and finally to provide guidance in using the sources.

There are, however, problems associated with using literature guides. The first and most important of these is that they are out of date as soon as they are published. The literature in any field is changing as the subject develops, new sources are constantly becoming available, and some sources are withdrawn, or changed in some way, perhaps by being transferred to a computerized system. A literature guide can therefore only reflect the state of the literature at a particular time. Another problem is that literature guides may be written for a particular audience, such as librarians and information scientists, and thus of less value to other readers, research workers or hospital doctors, say, because they assume too much knowledge on the part of the reader and miss out details needed by inexperienced literature searchers. Another feature to be aware of is that of bias. All books reflect the bias of their authors and a particular problem that can arise from literature guides is a bias towards the author's country of origin. For example, a book with a bias towards the United States will be of only limited value to a research worker in a developing country. And, of course, guides can contain errors: they may omit important sources, give incorrect bibliographic citations and, as already mentioned, fail to provide up-to-date information on changing sources.

There are three important standard reference tools that are frequently used at the beginning of a literature search.

Guide to reference material. 4th edition. Vol. 1, *Science and technology.* Ed. by A. J. Walford. (London: Library Association, 1980.)

This standard reference work is in three volumes. Medicine is assigned its own section in the first volume. This section contains a selected bibliography of medical works under headings such as 'Medical libraries', 'Yearbooks' and 'Data tables'. Its coverage is not as extensive as that of more specialized books such as *Health sciences information sources* (discussed later). The index is a combined subject, author and title index.

Guide to reference books. 9th edition. Edited by E. P. Sheehy. (Chicago: American Library Association, 1976. Supplements 1980, 1982, 1984.)

This useful tool is divided into sections and provides both general information of interest to medical information seekers (general reference works including newspapers, government publications, dissertations) and specifically medical works under the headings medicine, dentistry, nursing, nutrition, pharmacology, public health, toxicology and veterinary medicine. Under each of these headings is a selected bibliography of key items.

Printed reference material. 2nd edition. Edited by Gavin L. Higgens. (London: Library Association, 1984.)

This work is relatively cheap and provides an overview of printed reference materials from the standpoint of type of material. There are chapters on all the major reference tools such as encyclopedias, maps, atlases and gazetteers. This book does not provide much information on specific medical information tools but it does provide a wealth of background information.

There are a number of important guides to the medical literature.

Information sources in the medical sciences. 3rd edition. Edited by L. T. Morton and S. Godbolt. (London: Butterworths, 1984.)

This guide is packed with useful information on medical information and covers printed, mechanized and audiovisual sources. The book is written by a series of contributors, each a medical librarian or subject specialist and active in his or her own particular field.

The book is divided into twenty-four chapters, of which seven are concerned with general aspects relating to information sources while the remainder are concerned with information sources covering a particular topic. This arrangement is useful as it enables the reader to choose between a general introduction and a specialized treatment of a particular topic. The general topics covered are: 'Libraries and their use'; 'Primary sources of information'; 'Indexes, abstracts, bibliographies and reviews'; 'Standard reference sources'; 'Mechanized sources of information retrieval'; 'Historical, biographical and bibliographic sources'; 'Organization of personal files'; and 'Audiovisual materials'. The latter chapter is a new feature of the third edition.

To take a sample chapter, 'Primary sources of information' by R. J. Dannatt, we find twenty-six clearly written pages divided by headings such as 'personal contacts', which discusses so-called invisible colleges (informal links for information exchange among researchers with similar interests, often on an international basis), Information Exchange Groups, and relatively up-to-date research on the use and exchange of information; 'the periodical literature'; 'developments in biomedical communication'; 'medical journals'; 'guides to journals'; and 'usage'. The last two of these sections together provide a comprehensive picture of the role of periodicals in medicine, their advantages and disadvantages, and how to find out about them. The chapter continues with the following headings: 'research reports'; 'theses'; 'translation facilities'; and 'current awareness'. It concludes with two useful appendices, which include a comprehensive list of guides to periodicals and other publications and also a list of 'biomedical periodicals' selected (a) as representing in 1970 all fields of clinical medicine; (b) as most frequently borrowed by other libraries from the British Library Lending Division in 1967; and (c) as most promptly and most frequently cited in 1972 by a group of twenty-one pathology journals selected from the *Science Citation Index* database. This listing provides a useful guide to biomedical periodicals and their relative values but is unfortunately based on out-of-date information.

This chapter does not provide comprehensive coverage of primary sources of information, and important omissions include patents, clinical notes and laboratory reports. Nor does it mention newer developments in the periodical literature, such as electronic journals (i.e. journals which are available on a computerized database to which authors can directly input text, which is then edited online, and finally read by readers who may themselves input their comments and queries onto the database).

The chapters on specialized topics cover anatomy and physiology, public health, tropical medicine, medical microbiology, general practice and many others. In the chapter on general practice, the section headings are 'indexes'; 'reviews and yearbooks'; 'journals'; 'monographs and textbooks'; 'education for general practice'; 'government and official statements'; 'statistics and research'; 'practice organization'; and 'history'. There is a wealth of detailed information contained in these sections. For example, the section on 'statistics and research' covers publications on general practice content and workload, collection of morbidity statistics, individual practice accounts, information from patients concerning their sickness, methods of research and classification. One slight problem that the user will find in connection with this chapter is that although it provides details of the most important publications up to 1984 it does *not* provide guidance on how to find out about future publications, something that the present book aims to do in section 1.8. The other chapters are arranged in a similar manner but with additional sections relevant to the subject under consideration; thus the chapter 'Pharmacology and therapeutics' includes sections on 'pharmacopoeias', 'drug indexes and compendia' and 'legal requirements'.

The subject index of this book includes subject headings, title headings for items mentioned in the text, names of organizations and services. It is clearly laid out and uses a variety of typescripts to distinguish between the different types of entry.

Health sciences information sources. By Ching-Chih Chen. (Cambridge, Massachusetts: MIT, 1981.)

This is another very important medical guidebook. It covers the U.S. literature in detail, as well as sources from other countries. It is a massive book almost 800 pages long and provides comprehensive coverage of medical and health sciences literature. It is arranged by type of information source and within each category by subject—the reverse arrangement to that in *Information sources in the medical sciences*. The clear contents pages indicate this arrangement and the following headings can be found here: selection tools; guides to the literature; bibliographies; encyclopedias; dictionaries; handbooks; tables, almanacs, databooks, statistical sources; manuals, laboratory manuals and workbooks, and sourcebooks; guides; atlases; directories, yearbooks, biographical sources; history;

important series and other reviews of progress; treatises; monographs; abstracts and indexes, and current-awareness services; periodicals; technical reports and government documents; conference proceedings, translations, dissertations, and research in progress, preprints and reprints; classification, standards and patents; trade literature; non-print materials; professional societies and their publications; and databases.

To take a particular section, such as that on 'Handbooks', there are thirty-two sub-sections ranging from 'general' and 'allergy and immunology' to 'veterinary medicine'. If we turn to the sub-section on 'psychiatry and psychology' then we find twenty-three entries in title order, each with a short description. All of the items in this particular section were published in the United States and, with the exception of series, all were published in the 1970s.

As another example, the chapter on 'Professional societies and their publications' provides a useful list of the directories that cover societies and associations, followed by a list of important American societies in subject order.

The author's information for this guide came from a number of important sources, which are listed at the beginning of the book. They include medical and scientific journals, non-medical and non-scientific journals (e.g. *Aslib Proceedings*), books and finally, published lists of 'core' medical literature. This list of sources provides a useful signpost to information seekers who wish to find out about new items.

At the end of this book, there is a comprehensive list of journal references on topics relevant to the health sciences. The references are arranged alphabetically by subject and it is slightly offputting to find that the subject arrangement is not the same as that used in the rest of the book. Thus items on abstracts, indexes and current-awareness services can be found under the following headings in the reference list:

Abstracts and indexes
Citation indexing and citations
Current-awareness services
Indexing and abstracting

It is really necessary to skim through all the subject headings in order to cover one's subject accurately. There is a useful author index to this reference list.

There are two additional indexes to this book, a title and an author index. However, although for each kind of information source items are arranged by subject, the book lacks a subject index. Anyone using this book to compile a list of sources on a particular topic has to be prepared to work through the contents pages to obtain the page numbers of all the sections covering that topic.

There are many other guides to aspects of the medical and associated literatures, for example:

Consumer health information: a guide to sources. By Alan M. Rees. (Littleton, Colorado: Libraries Unlimited, 1980.)
   This is a selective guide to health care information sources that are available to the public. It covers topics such as cancer, drugs and drug abuse, and women and health. Its coverage is chiefly American.

Information sources in the history of science and medicine. Edited by Pietro Corsi and Paul Weindling. (London: Butterworths, 1983.)
   This is an authoritative and detailed guide to the literature on its subject and it covers

the historical development of science and medicine and of research methods, and describes the major libraries and archives. Technical, cultural and social aspects of science and medicine are all covered. The book is intended for an international readership and includes chapters on American, Islamic, Indian and Chinese science and medicine.

Virology: an information profile. Robin Nicholas and David Nicholas. (London: Mansell, 1983.)

This guide should prove to be of use to librarian, information scientist and research worker. It is clearly laid out in the following sections: 'History and scope of virology'; 'Organizations and their role in virology'; 'Conferences'; 'The literature of virology'; 'Searching the literature'; 'Culture collections'; and 'Legislation and safety'. It contains a comprehensive bibliography and also a directory of organizations, culture collections and libraries. The strengths of this book lie in its detailed coverage of a narrow subject area, good indexing and its ease of use, helped by its different styles and sizes of typeface.

An important point to remember is that many guides exist both to specific subjects and also to particular types of information source. These guides can be used to facilitate a literature search in a known subject area, or when moving to a new subject. They can save the information searcher time and help him or her to focus quickly on the most appropriate information sources.

1.2 Dictionaries

The function of a dictionary is to define and standardize the vocabulary in a subject field or language. Dictionaries in a particular subject field are particularly useful when searching for information as they can be used to obtain a quick and accurate understanding of a subject, its concepts, processes and techniques.

Subject dictionaries

In medicine both general and specific dictionaries exist. The main general medical dictionaries will be found in almost any good medical library:

Black's medical dictionary. 34th edition. Edited by William A. R. Thomson (London: A. & C. Black, 1984.)

The latest edition of this authoritative reference book to medical terms includes ninety new sections covering subjects such as glue sniffing, giggle micturition and white hair. The entries include definitions, explanations, therapy and diagnosis, and the dictionary has 461 illustrations and many tables.

It is a simple work to use, as main subject headings are printed in bold typescript followed by the entry. If necessary the user is directed from the subject heading to the preferred term which is associated with the entry; for example, RETENTION OF URINE (*see* URINE, RETENTION OF). In fact, a useful network of cross-references throughout the text direct the user to related subjects. For example, the entry under SALINES includes cross-references to PURGATIVES and ISOTONIC, while that under PURGATIVES includes references to CONSTIPATION and ABDOMEN, DISEASES OF.

Butterworths medical dictionary. 2nd edition. Edited by Macdonald Critchley. (London: Butterworths, 1978.)

The latest edition of this standard dictionary includes over 8,000 new entries. The entries include definitions, explanations, pronunciations and derivations but lack illustrations and tables. Although bold face is used to make the subject headings and subsidiary headings stand out, the overall format appears cramped.

There is substantial cross-referencing throughout the text and large-size typescript is used to distinguish cross-references from the body of the text.

Dorland's illustrated medical dictionary. 26th edition. (Philadelphia: W. B. Saunders, 1974.)

This dictionary contains over 120,000 entries, which include definitions, descriptions, pronunciations, derivations, tables and illustrations. The work is clearly laid out with bold-face subject headings. Cross-references refer the reader from a non-preferred to a preferred term (e.g. AFTERCATARACT, AFTER-CATARACT *see under* CATARACT) and also to related subjects.

Illustrated Stedman's medical dictionary. 24th edition. (Baltimore: Williams & Wilkins, 1982).

This dictionary lists current terminology as well as eponyms, acronyms and abbreviations. Each entry includes definitions, descriptions, pronunciations and plural forms. This is an extremely clearly laid-out book; labelled notches in the pages enable the user quickly to identify the appropriate alphabetical section. Cross-references take the user to preferred terms and also related subjects.

It is frequently necessary to use a variety of dictionaries when checking up on the meaning of a particular word. This is indicated in the following sample search.

Example search using general medical dictionaries

Search term   SICKLE-CELL ANAEMIA

Black's medical dictionary
Found under   SICKLE-CELL ANAEMIA
               Four sentences of explanation
               No cross-references
               Cross-referenced from ANAEMIA

Butterworths medical dictionary
Found under   ANAEMIA
               Sickle-cell anaemia hidden in six columns of text
               Two sentences of explanation
               No cross-reference from SICKLE-CELL ANAEMIA

Dorland's illustrated medical dictionary
Found under   ANEMIA
               Sickle-cell anemia hidden in four columns of text
               Two long sentences of explanation
               Cross-references to SICKLE-CELL–THALASSEMIA DISEASE
               Cross-referenced from SICKLEMIA

Illustrated Stedman's medical dictionary
Found under   SICKLEMIA (two sentences)
                    ANEMIA, SICKLE-CELL (nine sentences)
                    No cross-reference under either entry
                    No cross-reference from SICKLE-CELL ANEMIA

This example indicates that when using dictionaries it is important to use a range of works, to be aware of British and American differences in spelling and punctuation, and to follow up cross-references. It is also important to be aware of synonyms and the effects of different filing rules (letter-by-letter versus word-by-word filing) on the arrangement of entries in a dictionary.

If one is searching for information on a specific subject then it is frequently necessary to use a specialized dictionary. Numerous specialized dictionaries exist and can be found using sources such as *Health sciences information sources* and *Information sources in the medical sciences* (discussed in section 1.1). When using any dictionary, but particularly a specialized one, it is worth while to check the following factors: (a) its date of publication; (b) the aims and objectives of the dictionary; (c) the authority of the compiler(s); and (d) the vocabulary—for example, how technical is the terminology it uses; and also the factors that have been mentioned previously: (e) physical arrangement; (f) spelling (British or American); (g) punctuation; (h) layout; (i) cross-references; (j) vocabulary control such as the use of synonyms as entry points; and (k) filing rules.
    Some examples follow, and will demonstrate these considerations in practice.

Dictionary of epidemiology. Edited by John M. Last. (Oxford: Oxford University Press, 1983.)
    This relatively new book is 'an attempt to bring some order to the occasionally chaotic nomenclature' and it appears to be aimed at workers at all levels in the field. It includes definitions of general terms such as health services as well as many specific concepts such as Bayes' theorem and digit preference. As such, it will be useful both to newcomers to the field of epidemiology and to established researchers. Its vocabulary is simple but concise and where necessary diagrams and tables are used to facilitate understanding. The publication of this book has been sponsored actively by the International Epidemiological Association, the list of contributors is impressive and there is a useful bibliography at the end which shows the sources used in compiling this dictionary.
    The arrangement of entries is alphabetical with subject headings in bold face. Spelling is U.S. standard, and there is no cross-reference from other spelling variations of a word. The following sequence of entries indicates the use of punctuation and filing rules:

BIAS
BIAS, ascertainment
BIAS, IN ASSUMPTION
BIAS IN AUTOPSY
BIAS, BERKSON'S
BIAS DUE TO CONFOUNDING
BIAS, DESIGN
BIAS, DETECTION

BIAS DUE TO DIGIT PREFERENCE
BIAS IN HANDLING OUTLIERS
:
:
:

The example indicates that both punctuation and non-important words are ignored in the filing sequence—unfortunately for the user, who may be unsure about whether a word is meaningful or not and must work through a long sequence of entries to make sure that none is missed. Thorough cross-referencing ensures that the reader is sent to the appropriate entry and where necessary synonyms are given in the text.

Medical terminology in hospital practice. Incorporating 'Medical terminology for radiographers'. 3rd edition. By Paul M. Davies. (London: Heinemann, 1978.)

The aim of this book, now in its third edition, is 'to help members and students of the nursing and paramedical professions in obtaining such knowledge of medical terminology as is of practical value and interest in their everyday work'. The book may also be of use of medical secretaries. The two compilers are experts in their fields of radiology and pathology, but it is possible that the book is limited by having been compiled by two people plus their everyday colleagues. By contrast, the *Dictionary of epidemiology* had more than sixty contributors from around the world. However, the compilers do list an impressive array of standard works and journals which they have consulted while preparing their book.

The arrangement within the dictionary is unusual in that it is by subject, with an alphabetical index at the end of the book. The divisions are: 'Introduction, general pathological processes'; 'Infective diseases'; 'Diseases of the various systems of the body and obstetric terms'; and 'Other types of diseases'. Each section is written in a straightforward manner using non-technical jargon. Words which are defined in the text are highlighted by the use of bold type.

The index is relatively easy to use; it contains cross-references from British spelling variants to the preferred U.S. version and also a certain amount of cross-referencing. Many of the entries have indented subheadings, which facilitates the finding of the term one is looking for. Proper names of organisms are printed in italics.

Despite its rather unusual arrangement, this dictionary does appear to satisfy its own objective of helping nursing and paramedical staff to understand medical terminology.

Language dictionaries

There are a number of different kinds of language dictionary of use to the medical information seeker.

Abbreviations and acronyms dictionaries may be general in coverage:

Acronyms, initialisms, and abbreviations dictionary. 6th edition. 3 vols. Edited by Ellen T. Crowley. (Detroit: Gale Research, 1978.)

Alternatively, they may be subject-specific:

Dictionary of abbreviations in medicine and health sciences. By Harold H. Hughes. (Lexington, Massachusetts: Lexington Books, 1977.) Despite being out of date, this is an extremely useful book that contains more than 12,000 entries and for each entry includes varying definitions, e.g.

MMF   magnetomotive force; maximum midexpiratory flow; Member of the Medical Faculty

It includes a very useful guide to searching for abbreviations and also to constructing abbreviations.

Abbreviations and acronyms dictionaries are frequently required when carrying out a search. They enable the user to obtain the full meaning of an abbreviation or acronym, and can be used either to answer a particular enquiry (for example, what does IFA mean?) or to enable the searcher to broaden a search by encompassing fuller terms in the search strategy, such as finding out that desamino-D-arginine vasopressin can be used when searching for DDAVP.

Thesauri and nomenclature are useful in searching information sources as they can help to clarify the meaning of a particular term, its correct name and variant names, and to suggest related terms that can also be used in the search. They again may be either general or specific. The most famous general thesaurus, of course, is:

Roget's thesaurus. By Robin A. Dutch. (London: Longman, 1972.)

In medicine, one of the important classification schemes is that of *Index Medicus*, MeSH, which is discussed in detail in section 1.10. A more specific example is:

Nomenclature and criteria for diagnosis of diseases of the heart and great vessels. 7th edition. New York Heart Association Criteria Committee. (Boston, Massachusetts: Little, Brown, 1973.)

Details of these and additional items can be found in *Health sciences information sources*, discussed in section 1.1.

There are numerous foreign-language general and medical dictionaries and these are particularly useful when searching foreign-language abstracting and indexing services as they enable the searcher to identify appropriate search terms. The following are typical examples.

English–French

English–French French–English dictionary of medical and biological terms. 2nd edition. By P. Lepine and P. R. Peacock. (Paris: Flammarion, 1975.)

French–English dictionary of physical medicine and rehabilitation. By H. and G. Kamenetz (Paris: Librairie Maloine, 1972.)

English–German

Dental-Wörterbuch. Dictionary of dental practice. By Herbert Bucksch. (Munich: Verlag Neuer Merker, 1970.)

Wörterbuch der Psychiatrie und medizinischen Psychologie. By Uive H. Peters. (Munich: Urban & Schwarzenberg, 1971.)

Other languages

Ika, Shika, Waei Hasuon Bunrei Jiten: Japanese–English medical–dental dictionary. By Ryutaro Yamauchi (Tokyo: Perikan, 1965.)

Russian–English medical dictionary. By U.B. Eliseenkov *et al.* (Moscow: Russian Language Publishers, 1975.)

A short English–Swahili medical dictionary. By T. H. White. (London: Churchill-Livingstone, 1978.)

More than two languages

Elsevier's medical dictionary in five languages. 2nd edition. By A. Sliosberg. (Amsterdam: Elsevier, 1975.)

Medical dictionary: medizinisches Wörterbuch: dictionnaire médical. 5th edition. Edited by Emanuel Veillan, revised and enlarged by Albert Nobel. (New York: Huber, 1977.)

A number of bibliographies of dictionaries are available to help the searcher find out whether or not a suitable dictionary exists. Two examples are:

Bibliography of interlingual scientific and technical dictionaries. 5th edition. (Paris: Unesco, 1969.)

A bibliography of scientific, technical and specialized dictionaries, polyglot, bilingual, unilingual. By C. W. Rechenbach and E. R. Garnete. (Washington, D.C.: Catholic University Press, 1969.)

1.3 Encylopedias

Encylopedias provide a vast store of knowledge on either a particular subject:

Encyclopedia of psychoanalysis. By Ludwig Eidelberg. (New York: Macmillan, 1968.)

or the universe:

Encyclopaedia Britannica. (Chicago: Encyclopaedia Britannica, 1975.)

The aim of encyclopedias is to provide their user with a concise summary of a particular topic. They have limited use as a medical information source because their revision and updating tends to be infrequent and it is not uncommon to find an encyclopedia ten years out of date. Other information sources, such as textbooks, monographs and reviews, provide a more satisfactory means of obtaining up-to-date information on a subject. Encyclopedias do, though, offer a means of obtaining a historical summary of a particular medical topic. A few additional relevant encyclopedias include:

McGraw-Hill encyclopedia of science and technology. 4th edition. (New York: McGraw-Hill, 1977.)

Penguin medical encyclopedia. 3rd edition. By P. Wingate. (Harmondsworth, Middlesex: Penguin, 1983.)

World Book illustrated home medical encyclopedia. (Chicago: World Book, 1979).

1.4 Directories

A directory is a reference tool that provides the user with information on people, enterprises or organizations. Directories act as signposts to other sources of information. They are one of the most useful kinds of tool found in a library as they frequently enable information searchers to make short cuts. For example, in searching for information on the topic 'microcomputer aids for the visually handicapped', it would be worth while to check to see whether any organizations exist which are concerned with this topic. If they do, then it would be worth contacting them; they may have ready-prepared bibliographies and information packs on the subject, which would save the searcher from having to carry out a literature review.

Finding out about directories

Directories of directories exist and can be used to track down relevant items.

Directory of directories. 2nd edition. By James M. Etheridge. (Detroit: Gale Research, 1983.)
   This directory is divided into three sections: the directory itself, a title index and a subject index. The directory section is split into two parts: general business directories, and specific industries and lines of business. Section 12 is concerned with health and medicine and it contains a straightforward alphabetical listing of medical and related directories. The entries show a heavy bias towards American publications. Information contained in each entry includes title, publisher (with address and telephone number), coverage, description of the entries, arrangement, indexes, number of pages, frequency and prices. The subject index is clearly laid out and there are numerous entries under 'medicine'.

When searching for a directory, it is wise not to rely totally on one information source and the *Directory of directories* can be used in conjunction with:

International bibliography of special directories. 7th edition. Edited by Helga Lengenfelder. (Munich: K. G. Saur, 1983.)
   This edition 'lists approximately 6,000 address books and membership lists published regularly or irregularly in some fifty countries worldwide'. It is split into the following sections: general directories; cultural affairs, arts, sciences and technology; state and society; commerce and industry; individuals; classified list of trades and industries; and public transportation and transport communication. This arrangement results in medical directories' being spread over numerous sections, and as the bibliography does not possess a subject or title index, searching can be quite tedious and time-consuming. However, as this source does provide information on directories not otherwise easily tracked down, it should not be dismissed.

A selection of important directories

It is beyond the scope of this book to discuss in detail all the directories of relevance to medicine. Below are a selection of some of the most important; other directories are discussed in detail elsewhere, for example in Chapter 3, 'Organizations and people'.

Aslib directory of information sources in the United Kingdom. 5th edition. Edited by Ellen M. Codlin. (London: Aslib, 1984.)

This is a useful starting point for anyone trying to locate specialized information sources on medicine (or any other subject, for that matter). Volume 2 covers the social sciences, medicine and the humanities, and it is an alphabetical listing of more than 3,600 organizations. The bodies included may be commercial companies, scientific and research organizations, learned and academic societies, service, governmental, negotiating, standardizing, qualifying, professional or amateur bodies, producers of data, statistics and abstracts, experts in specialized fields, and repositories of large and very small collections of books. The subject index indicates that a vast range of medical topics are covered, from burn injuries to psychosomatic medicine. There is a useful abbreviations index too.

Directory of British associations. 7th edition. (Beckenham, Kent: CBD Research, 1982.)

This directory provides information on national associations, societies, institutes and similar organizations. It includes many organizations of interest to medical workers, such as the Guild of Catholic Doctors, the Irish Medical Association and the Scottish Society for History and Medicine. In particular, it includes many voluntary organizations and self-help groups, for example the Haemophilia Society and the Parkinson's Disease Society. The arrangement within the book is alphabetical by name and there is a subject index.

Directory of European scientific associations. (Part 1: *National trade and professional associations*, 3rd edition, 1981; Part 2: *National learned, scientific and technical associations*, 2nd edition, 1979.) (Beckenham, Kent: CBD Research.)

This directory provides information on numerous European scientific associations. Like its companion, the *Directory of British associations*, it is extremely simple to use. If you require information on an association or associations in a particular field, look in the subject index (printed on bright red paper) to find the number of the appropriate subject heading; for example, 'Medical practitioners' is 4600. Then turn to the main text and find the subject heading. Under it associations are arranged by countries.

For information on a specific association, turn to the alphabetical index of organizations. After the name of the association will be found the number of the appropriate subject heading, together with the country designation. The entry for this association can then be found. If an abbreviation of its name but not the full name is known, the abbreviations index will give the full name, subject heading and number, and country designation.

Directory of international and national medical and related societies. By G. Zeitak and F. Berman. (Oxford: Pergamon, 1982.)

This directory covers the kinds of organization suggested by its title and also voluntary and professional bodies. It is computer-produced and has poor-quality print. Entries include the following information: name (in English and the original language), address, telephone/telex number, subject category, number of members, publications, dates and location of meetings, and are arranged by country. There are country, name and subject indexes.

To find a particular item, for example an organization that deals with cystic fibrosis in Israel, turn to the subject index. There is the following entry under 'Cystic fibrosis':

Cystic fibrosis
:
:
Israel 324–006

Then turn to the main body of the directory and find the country heading, work through the numerical codes and at 324–006 the following entry is found:

324–006–5 (0148)
Cystic fibrosis research assn. Israel
POB 31171
TEL-AVIV, ISRAEL
TEL. 03–773103
MEMBERS: 500   SUBJECTS 80
PUBS: NEWS ISRAEL CYS FIBROSIS FOUNDATION

The numerical code indicates the country, position of entry in the country listing and the source of information for the entry, as for example from a returned questionnaire.

The subject index is in three sections: a thesaurus of subject headings; a key to subject codes (eighty codes have been assigned to the whole field of medicine); and the subject index proper. This latter is very complicated and detracts from the usefulness of the guide.

Encyclopedia of associations. 14th edition. Edited by Nancy Yakes and Denise Akey. (Detroit, Michigan: Gale Research, 1980.)

This is the American equivalent of the *Directory of British associations*, mentioned above, and it is published in three volumes. Volume 1, *National organizations of the U.S.*, is the volume most commonly found in libraries. Its entries are arranged by subject and it has over 100 pages of medical and related associations. Entries are chiefly U.S.-based bodies and they cover numerous subject areas, two examples being the Society of United States Air Force Flight Surgeons and the American Academy of Maxillofacial Prosthetics. The index includes both names of organizations and subject keywords, interfiled. The result of this combination is a massive index which needs detailed skimming in order to find the appropriate entry.

Volume 2 is a geographic and executive index while volume 3 is a periodical supplement of new associations and projects. The last volume is particularly useful as it enables the searcher to track down new organizations which are unlikely to have entries in other directories.

Health sciences information sources, discussed in detail in section 1.1, is another important directory which includes a detailed listing of medical organizations.

Help! I need somebody. A guide to national associations for people in need. 3rd edition. By Sally Knight. (London: Kimpton, 1980.)

This useful directory covers more than 700 U.K. organizations which help people (or their relatives or friends) who have a specific medical or social problem. The arrangement is alphabetical and the name of the organization is in bold type. Below is a typical example:

14 Medical information: a profile

>**150 CHARIOT,** 17 Wood Lane,
> Streetly, SUTTON COLDFIELD,
> West Midlands B74 3LP
> Tel: 021-353-3057 (Provides
> transport for severely disabled,
> bedfast and chairfast people
> in the Midlands.)

The subject index relates subject with entry number, e.g.

>Physically handicapped
>:
>:
> transport/travel for 150, ...

Medical research directory (Chichester: John Wiley, 1983).
 This book covers current and recent research in the fields of medicine and nursing in universities, polytechnics, colleges, hospitals and research establishment. Information is organized under forty-five broad subject entries and the following is a typical entry:

>Anatomy
>245 Newcastle Health Authority,
>   Scottish Life House, 2–10
>   Archbold Terrace, Newcastle
>   upon Tyne NE2 1EF
>
> 1 Hall R.R Mr—Scanning electron
>   microscopy in the study of
>   premalignant and malignant changes
>   in the urothelium of the bladder
>   (Newcastle Health Authority)
>   Newcastle upon Tyne—Freeman
>   Hospital—Urology.

It gives the organization and within organization entries by name of researcher, title of research project and the source of funding, and the location of the research.

Medical research index. 5th edition. (Harlow: Longman, 1979.)
 This useful publication covers international research establishments and research which is carried out in over 130 countries. Arrangement is by country, and within a country by name. There are two volumes, the second being a comprehensive index of organizations.

The above three examples can all be used when searching for information on medical research and they are complemented by the British publication *Research in British universities, polytechnics and colleges*: Vol. 2, *Biological sciences*, which is described in detail in section 1.12.

Self-help and the patient: a directory of national organizations concerned with various diseases and handicaps. 8th edition. (London: Patient Association, 1982.)
 This lists organizations that give individuals information and advice on particular diseases or physical or mental handicaps. Coverage is limited and organizations are listed under the following headings: addictions, children—parents, deafness, mental disability

and emotional problems, physical disabilities and handicaps, sight disabilities, specific disorders and problems, women. There is an index.

World of learning 1983–1984. 34th edition. (London: Europa, 1983.)

This important directory provides ready access to detailed information about academies, learned societies, research institutes, libraries and archives, museums and art galleries, and universities and colleges for individual countries throughout the world. Arrangement is by country, and it is possible to obtain a relatively clear picture of any country's information sources by looking at the appropriate section. There is also a useful section on international organizations.

This book is easy to use. Searching can be carried out via country, or by the index to institutions. If one is carrying out a subject search then it is necessary to work through the individual country sections, which are arranged by type of organization and within that by subject or name. This can be time-consuming.

This is a key directory which should not be overlooked when searching for information on organizations.

Yearbook of international organisations 1983/1984. 20th edition. Edited by the Union of International Associations. (Munich: K. G. Saur, 1983.)

This mammoth yearbook covers about 15,000 organizations which are 'truly international', by which is meant active in at least three countries. Individual entries are extremely detailed and are arranged by an entry number in one of thirteen sections according to the type of organization. It is impossible to use this book without using the main index, which includes names, name keywords and organization abbreviations or initials. Once the appropriate body has been found in the index, the entry can be found by means of its entry number. The book is slow and cumbersome to use as a result of this arrangement, which is not helped by the dense, tightly packed typeface.

The above examples should enable the information searcher to find out about organizations of interest to medical and allied workers. It would be wrong to think that these are the only generalized directories in existence. There are many more, and also many specialized directories. *Health sciences information sources* lists over twenty pages of directories and they include examples such as:

Bioenergy directory. The Bioenergy Council. (Washington, D.C.: Bioenergy Council, 1978.)

Directory for exceptional children. 8th edition. Porter Sargent staff *et al.* (Boston, Massachusetts: Porter Sargent, 1978.)

Directory of agencies serving the visually handicapped in the United States. 20th edition. American Foundation for the Blind. (New York: American Foundation of the Blind, 1978.)

However, the majority of medical libraries cannot afford to keep many specialized directories. They tend to purchase general, standard tools and buy specialized directories only if they are relevant to the specific needs of their users. Thus specialized directories are most likely to be found in the very large medical libraries, large national libraries and in specialized libraries or information units.

There are many directories which enable one to find out about people. The majority of professional bodies, such as the Pharmaceutical Society, publish membership lists, which are useful sources.

The *Medical register* is published annually by Britain's General Medical Council, and it is the official register of personnel qualified to practise medicine in the United Kingdom. In practice, one tends to use the *Medical directory*, which is published annually by Churchill. This is a useful sourcebook since it contains details of medical schools and hospitals in the United Kingdom, short biographies of members of the profession who are registered with the GMC, giving degrees, medical school attended, current position, previous posts and professional publications.

Most countries have equivalent publications (the *American medical directory* is an example) and there is a general international publication:

International medical who's who. (London: Longman, 1980.)

This provides details of over 12,000 people from more than 120 countries. It is in two volumes. The entries are detailed and include details of professional interests, current appointment and present unpaid offices.

1.5 Handbooks and databooks

Handbooks and databooks are reference books which provide brief and factual information. In the field of medicine, they include information such as chemical and physical tables, dosages, toxicities, drug interactions, normal values and statistical trends. They are available in many subject fields and enable one to answer brief factual enquiries.

Information on handbooks and databooks relevant to medicine and allied topics can be obtained from sources such as *Health sciences information sources*, *Information sources in the medical sciences* and *Printed reference material*.

When using these information sources it is worth while to bear the following criteria in mind:

1. How up-to-date is the information?
2. Is there likely to be a more up-to-date source available?
3. Who produced this information?
4. How has this information been produced?
5. Have the data been standardized or normalized?
6. What units and definitions are used in the book?
7. Has the information been validated?
8. Is it possible to double-check the information using a different source? If so, are the same results obtained?

When searching handbooks and databooks, always check your information with another source.

Handbooks and databooks can be categorized according to subject. Below we will investigate a sample of sources in two areas, the fields of drug information and statistics.

Drug information handbooks and databooks

Martindale: the extra pharmacopoeia. 28th edition. (London: The Pharmaceutical Press, 1982.)

The current edition of this databook, at the time of writing, is the twenty-eighth, which was published in 1982, one hundred years after the first edition.

Martindale must be known by every medical librarian, pharmacist and general practitioner in the United Kingdom and many other countries. It is very useful for giving quick answers when a question of formulation dose or side-effect is posed. The 28th edition, and the currency of its information, is a superb example of how the use of a computer can aid information dissemination. For example, the 'monograph' for Benoxaprofen (Opren) includes references to the withdrawal of the product from the market—a withdrawal that occurred only two months prior to *Martindale*'s publication.

As in earlier editions, the text is divided into three parts. Part 1 contains 'monographs' on 3,000 substances. Drugs of similar action are brought together; for example, one of the 105 chapters covers 'Antineoplastic agents'. In this and other chapters there is a detailed introduction to the subject before the focus shifts to individual agents.

Part 2 comprises short 'monographs' mainly on new drugs which are not easily classified or are under investigation, or obsolescent ones that are nevertheless still of interest such as bradykinin.

The third and final part is concerned with the composition of over 900 over-the-counter proprietary medicines such as Germoloids and Lloyd's cream. Interestingly this section also covers toothpastes containing fluoride. There is an excellent directory section covering every manufacturer of products mentioned throughout the text and giving names and addresses in full.

There are three indexes. Users should first turn to the general index, which is well cross-referenced. As a space-saving measure, the long lists of pharmaceutical forms have been omitted but this in no way detracts from the usefulness of the index. The second index refers to clinical use, and is useful in the way it gathers together medicinal products used to treat similar conditions. Thus quinine can be sought under the general index entries at 'Q' or can be identified when looking for drugs to treat night cramp as a clinical condition. The final index is of *Martindale* identity numbers, a feature that will be of use mainly with the associated online service.

Martindale is a superb drug information store, excellently presented and up to date. As it is published only once every five years, the online version will be particularly useful for purposes of updating as well as for finding answers to complex queries. The online version will be described in section 2.7.

ABPI Data Sheet Compendium, 1984–85. (London: Pharmind, 1984.)

Data sheets are issued for each licensed medicinal product in order to comply with the (British) Medicines Act of 1968. They are prepared by individual pharmaceutical companies and vary somewhat in style. All must contain a minimum amount of information. However, data sheets from the majority of pharmaceutical companies are compiled annually into the *ABPI Data Sheet Compendium*. It contains, in addition to the data sheets, a number of pieces of information concerning the marketing and consumption of medicinal products. First is the code of practice for the pharmaceutical industry, which makes very interesting reading. The data sheets follow this and are arranged alphabetically by the title of the drug company. Following the data sheets is a section entitled 'Physiological values for some body fluids', which is a reprint of pages from the *Pharmaceutical handbook* and other sources. Tables representing desirable weights for men and women are included, as is a table of obstetric data. The exact relevance of these tables and data in relation to the data sheets is not at first apparent—most users of the source would tend to turn elsewhere for such information—but for some people the extra information may prove useful. The *Compendium* is supplied free of charge, which makes it very acceptable.

A list of new products which appear in the current *Compendium* for the first time precedes the main indexes. The first index, the 'Index of products', is an alphabetical index of preparations listed using their trade or proprietary name. It is followed by an index of non-proprietary products, which gives the name or names of proprietary preparations that contain the product. The two indexes would be better merged, though the non-proprietary index can be useful to trace the name of a proprietary product when only the approved name is known.

At the end of the book is a directory of participating companies with their names and addresses.

MIMS—Monthly Index of Medical Specialities. (London: Medical Publications.)

In all general practitioner surveys concerning sources of information, *MIMS* is always voted the most useful source, particularly in alerting a general practitioner to new products. It is sent free of charge to full-time general practitioners, heads of hospital pharmacy departments and on rotation to others. Its basic use is as an *aide mémoire* but it is often cited as a source of drug interactions and contraindications. There are various lists in *MIMS* such as a directory of manufacturers, a list of deleted products and one of name changes. There is a pharmacological index covering major body systems and diseases, and this leads the user to the relevant section within *MIMS*. (Since 1 April 1985, *MIMS* has added a symbol [x in a square] to products which have been placed on the black list and are not available for prescribing on National Health Service prescriptions.) The non-proprietary index gives products containing given non-proprietary names either as the sole ingredient or as part of a compound. For example, Amitriptyline is the sole ingredient of Tryptizol but is also an ingredient of Limbitrol. Both are included under the non-proprietary name Amitriptyline, Limbitrol being marked with an asterisk to indicate its compound nature. The main alphabetical index, which has entries for diseases and product names, is at the back of *MIMS*.

Advertising is scattered throughout *MIMS*, as are comments which act as reminders and cross-references. Codes used within the product lists indicate prescribing details. Details of special precautions, contra-indications, form (e.g. film-coated) etc. are included with entries. The basic arrangement within *MIMS* is by pharmacological activity.

Statistical handbooks and databooks

Information on statistical sources can be obtained by using guides to the statistical literature. Important ones include:

Guide to official statistics. 4th edition. (HMSO: Central Statistical Office, 1982.)

This guide sets out 'to give the user a broad indication of whether the statistics he wants have been compiled and, if so, where they have been published'. It is extremely well laid out and information of interest to medical and associated workers can be found under the following headings: 'general'; 'population, vital statistics'; 'social statistics'; 'production industries'; and 'distribution and other services'. The subject index at the end of the book indicates twenty entries under the heading 'medical' and if we turn to the entry for 'primary health care services' we find seventeen sources divided into regular sources (14) such as *Scottish health statistics*, and occasional sources (3) such as *Primary health care in Inner London*. At the end of this publication, there is a useful list of U.K. government department contact points.

The equivalent American publication is:

Guide to U.S. government statistics. 4th edition. John Androit. (McLean, Virginia: Documents Index, 1973.)

More general guides include:

Directory of international statistics: Vol. 1, *United Nations*. (New York: United Nations, 1981.)

Statistics sources: a subject guide to data on industrial, business, social, educational and financial and other topics for the United States and internationally. By P. Wasserman and J. O'Brien. (Detroit, Michigan: Gale Research, 1980.)

Statistical sources can be divided into two main groups: government statistical sources and commercial medical market research services. Information on government statistical sources can be found using sources such as guides to government publications, government publishers' catalogues, etc. and is reasonably well documented. It is more difficult to track down statistics derived from non-governmental sources such as societies and charities, and these statistics may be published in report format and not widely distributed. It is always worth while to contact an organization in order to see whether it publishes statistical reports. An example of an established statistical source from an association is:

Facts about nursing. (New York: American Nurses' Association, 1935–.) Annual.
This publication includes statistical summaries of nursing distribution, education, economic status, professional organizations and allied health professionals.

This item was traced using *Health sciences information sources*, and it is in fact frequently necessary to use national bibliographies when searching for statistical sources.
Information from commercial medical market research services rarely enters traditional libraries or information units as it is extremely expensive. For a researcher who thinks that the information he or she is seeking is likely to be available from such a company, it is probably advisable to contact likely companies direct.
If, when searching for statistical information, you find it impossible to identify the most appropriate source then it is worth while to contact a library that specializes in statistical information. In the United Kingdom such a library is:

Statistics and Market Intelligence Library
Department of Trade and Industry
1 Victoria Street
London SW1H 0ET
England
(Tel: 01-215 5444/5445)

while in the United States there is the

Department of Commerce Library
14th and Constitution Avenue
NW, Washington, DC 20230

1.6 Patents

An important source of information that is frequently overlooked by medical workers is the patent literature. It contains a wealth of technical detail which is frequently not published in any other form. Even when it is, the information will often have been first available as a patent.

A patent is an agreement, normally between a government or its agency and an inventor, in which the inventor obtains a limited monopoly while the government receives information on the invention. The inventor must submit a detailed specification of the invention, to a level of description such that a reader of the patent should be able to repeat the invention. It is this specification that is the source of much useful technical information.

The following categories of invention are of interest to medical workers:

Products   e.g. synthetic chemical compounds such as Ampicillin, fermentation products and products of nature such as Cephalosporin C, microbial enzymes, microorganisms, viruses and cell lines.

Compositions   e.g. chemical compositions, pharmaceutical compositions, and biological compositions such as a mixed culture inoculent.

Processes   e.g. chemical microbiological processes.

Methods of use/treatment   e.g. treatment of a raw material in a pharmaceutical plant. Generally speaking methods of direct treatment of human subjects are patentable provided they are divorced from primary medical care. This means that therapeutic, diagnostic and surgical methods are unpatentable under most countries' laws. One important exception is the United States, where such methods can be patented.

The types of invention likely to be of interest to medical information seekers include pharmaceutical products and processes, microbiological products and processes, medical equipment, and aids for the handicapped and sick.

There are three main methods of searching the patent literature: using tools provided by patent offices, using secondary sources such as Ringdoc or *Chemical Abstracts*, or by using online patent information services.

Information tools provided by patent offices

Patent offices are found in most countries. Japan, West Germany, the United Kingdom and the United States each have their own office, and there is also a European Patent Office. Each country has its own patent system and publishes its own tools to help users to search the patent literature. A typical example which will be considered in detail is that of the United Kingdom's Patent Office.

All patents have certain distinguishing features: a unique patent number, a patent application number, date of filing, priority date, date application published, international classification code, local classification code, field of search code, applicant's name, inventor's name, agent's name and address. It is possible to search for patents by a variety of routes, as for example name of patent holder, subject of patent, or by patent number.

Searching by name (of the patent owner) is the simplest type of patent search. Each patent office produces its own name index. The United Kingdom's Patent Office, for example, publishes a book called *Names of applicants* for every 250,000 patent specifications, which lists the patents in order of patent owner. If you want to find out what patents the Wellcome Foundation owns then look through all the issues under this name, noting the numbers. You can then look up the full specifications. Each entry shows the owner, inventor(s), short title, class number and the patent number. Below is an example entry:

Wellcome Foundation Ltd. (Almedide)

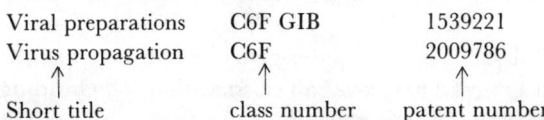

Viral preparations	C6F GIB	1539221
Virus propagation	C6F	2009786
↑	↑	↑
Short title	class number	patent number

Searching by subject matter varies slightly depending on which country's patents are being searched. It normally involves the following processes: identify the subject code; search through the subject indexes and obtain the patent numbers; read the abstracts/abridgements; select and obtain the relevant patents. The following example indicates how to search for U.K. patents by subject. The U.K. Patent Office breaks down the subject matter of all inventions into eight sections, A–H, which are themselves subdivided many times. The breakdown is as follows:

- A. human necessities
- B. performing operations
- C. chemistry, metallurgy
- D. textiles, paper
- E. civil engineering, building accessories
- F. mechanics, lighting, heating
- G. instrumentation
- H. electricity

The subject approach involves a number of steps. First the searcher should look up the subject in the Catchwords Index, which relates keywords to the classification code. This index must be used with care and the subject should be approached via a number of related terms and synonyms to prevent the classification code from being missed. Then he or she should turn to the Classification Key, where over four hundred subject matter fields are identified and defined. These headings are grouped into divisions; Divisions A5–6 are concerned with medicine and surgery, as well as fire fighting and entertainment. Each division is then broken down into detailed codes. It is frequently necessary to search through several places in the Classification Key in order to find the correct classification code. The Patent Office has published a number of useful guides to its Classification Key, viz. *Structure of the Classification Key, Notes on the use of the Classification Key* and *Heading UIS Universal Indexing Schedules for use, application, utility and property*. A useful tip when trying to find the right classification code for a particular search is to start with a known patent on that subject, obtain the classification code from the front of the patent and then check that code in the Classification Index.

Once the classification code has been obtained then the searcher can proceed by using what are called Subject-Matter File-Lists, which are lists of patent specifications (identified by their serial patent number) to which have been assigned a particular classification number. There are three kinds of Subject-Matter File-Lists.

Series A File-Lists cover all the patents published in the United Kingdom from 1911 up to patent number 1,000,000 (July 1965). It is worth noting that these lists are organized according to the Classification Key in force in 1965, and this older Classification Key must be used when searching through this particular file-list.

Series C and Series D File-Lists are computer-generated on request from the United Kingdom's Patent Office. They cover all classification code headings for patent number 1,000,001 onwards and selected headings prior to specification number 1,000,000. Series C File-Lists are available for any single classification code mark. In contrast, Series D File-Lists are available for combinational searches of two or more code marks, up to a practical limit of 100 code-marks. Relationships between subjects can be expressed using Boolean logic, i.e. AND, OR and NOT.

Subject codes can also be used to select the appropriate sections of the weekly *Abstracts Pamphlet Service* to scan. Here patents are grouped into twenty-five units of the Classification Key to facilitate scanning. Within each unit the patent abstracts are arranged serially by patent number. Annual cumulations of the abstracts service are available. It is worth noting that a synonym for abstracts is 'abridgement' and the patent literature tends to discuss abridgements rather than abstracts.

As an example, let us take a patent search of U.K. patents on artificial legs. To identify the class number of this subject turn to the Catchwords Index. The required entry is found under the heading 'Leg(s),' and if this subject had been approached via 'prosthetic devices' or 'artificial legs' then the Index would have provided no guidance to the appropriate heading. The entry looks like this:

LEG(S)
   appliances for measuring legs   G1M
      :
      :
      :
   artificial legs   A5R
      :
      :
      ;

Then turn to the Classification Definitions section, which lists—under the entry A5R Medicine, surgery, dentistry, etc.—what is included and excluded at this code. Next one should turn to the *Patent abridgements*, which are bound volumes arranged in blocks of 25,000 or 50,000 patents by class number. Select the volume which contains the block of patents for A5R. At the front of this volume is a detailed Classification Key and one can search this to find the specific class number. The following entry will be found:

A5R   Part F

   R25A   framework and casings
   R25B1   hip
   R25B2   knee
   R25C   operating and controlling means

Having got the appropriate class number, say R25A, go to the next section of the volume, the 'subject matter index', which is a computer printout list of the subclasses and then patent numbers, e.g.

   A5   R25A
        2064331
        2067074
        2069847

Then turn to the abridgements/abstracts, which are arranged in patent number order, and look at the relevant entries. This exercise must be repeated by going through all the relevant volumes. It is important to check the classification in the front of each volume, as it changes from time to time.

This type of manual subject search is very time-consuming. A quicker method of searching is either to buy from the U.K. Patent Office a computer printout of all the patent numbers in the class of interest to you, or to carry out an online search as described in Chapter 2. To obtain a Patent Office computer printout it is necessary first to ascertain the required class number of interest and this involves using either the current key (for File-List B, which covers patents to date back to number 1,000,000) or the key that was in force at the time of patents numbered in the range 960,000–1,000,000 which is covered by File-List A. Then contact the U.K. Patent Office, request the appropriate computer printout(s) and pay the necessary fee. It will take about a fortnight to get the list. Once you have obtained the numbers it is possible to check the relevant abridgements to see if the patents are what you were looking for, and then look at the full texts.

It is possible to carry out a more specific search if you are looking for patents which fall into more than one subject area. You can request a File-List D, which covers patents falling in more than one subject area, and you can request a particular search using class numbers linked by Boolean logic operators (AND, OR, NOT).

The explanation given so far relates to searching for patents that have already been published. Patents are constantly being applied for and published and to keep up to date with U.K. patents one must use a weekly publication called *Official Journal (Patents)* which lists patent applications and those which have been published. These are arranged in subject matter order and a name index is also provided in the journal. Once one has identified the relevant patent then it is possible to obtain a copy of either the application or the published patent.

Other countries handle their patent publications in much the same way as the United Kingdom's Patent Office. Patents are published and name indexes and classification keys are available. Some countries, like the United States, only publish the patent once it has been accepted as an invention; other countries, such as France, West Germany or the U.S.S.R., publish both before and after the patent has been examined by the Patent Office. The European Patent Convention and the Patent Co-operation Treaty have resulted in patents being processed and published in a similar way through the European Patent Office and World Intellectual Property Organization.

In the United Kingdom, comprehensive patent collections, including foreign patents, are held in the Science Reference Library in London and also a range of provincial public libraries which form part of the Patents Information Network.

Secondary sources

Several important abstracting and indexing services cover the patent literature. The most important services are those provided by Derwent Publications Ltd. in London. Derwent's literature abstracting services include:

Biotechnology Abstracts   1982–
Chemical Reactions Documentation Service   1975–
Pestdoc   1968–   (covers pesticides)
Ringdoc   1964–   (covers drugs)
Vetdoc   1968–   (covers veterinary drugs)

The information is supplied with detailed abstracts, controlled keywords and subject codes. These services are available not only in printed format but also on magnetic tapes, microfiche and film, and may be accessed online.

The above services cover the patent as well as the journal literature, but the following Derwent services are solely concerned with the patent literature.

World Patents Index (WPI) (1974–) provides titles and bibliographic details but no abstracts. It is printed as a weekly journal and covers all countries according to topic, patentee and subject matter. Cumulated indexes are available on microfiche.

World Patents Abstracts (WPA) (1975–) is a weekly journal of patent abstracts with drawings that are classified by country into separate publications, including *British Patents Abstracts, German Patents Gazette, United States Patents Abstracts* and *European Patents Reports*. Patents are arranged by Derwent classification codes, which include codes for 'pharmaceuticals', 'personal and domestic' and 'health and amusement'. *WPA* also includes subject-orientated weekly journals for non-chemical technologies.

Central Patents Index (CPI) (1970–) provides documentation of chemically related patents in alerting bulletins, basic abstracts journals, profile booklets and coded cards (and also microfilm, microfiche and magnetic tapes).

Derwent Publications Ltd. thus provides an extremely comprehensive patent information service. Its services are extremely up to date and on average the abstracts are published by Derwent some four to seven weeks after their date of issue. Further information about its ever-developing information services can be obtained from: Derwent Publications Ltd., Rochdale House, 128 Theobalds Road, London WC1X 8RP, England.

The general abstracting and indexing services, such as *Chemical Abstracts* and *Current Biotechnology Abstracts*, do cover patents and may be of use in a patent information search when specialized sources are not available.

Online patent information sources

Online databases that specifically cover patents include *CA Patents, CLAIMS/CHEM, CLAIMS/CLASS, CLAIMS/U.S. Patents, INP1, Ringdoc, World Patent Latest* and *WP1*. Online databases are dealt with in Chapter 2.

1.7   Report literature

Reports really developed as information sources during and following the second world war. They are documental evidence to support work carried out for government, industry or academia. Most reports concern science and technology in some form, and medicine figures as an important area of consideration.

Many institutions produce reports as the first indication of work carried out prior to a paper being published. The report will contain much more detail than a paper, and will show negative as well as positive results. The pharmaceutical industry and certain government departments and funded agencies produce reports, or sponsor other institutions to produce them. In the medical sciences, while the scientific paper is a generally preferred method of disseminating information, bodies such as the World Health Organization do use the report widely. That particular organization will supply on demand a list of its publications, and tracing other reports is often best done using a similar technique (that is, by simply writing to ask the organization concerned). In Britain, HMSO provides lists of published reports. The American Hospital Association (AHA) publishes a list with abstracts entitled *Abstracts of Published Reports* (Chicago: AHA). The British Library produces *British Reports, Translations and Theses Received by BLLD*.

British Reports, Translations and Theses. (Boston Spa: British Library.)

This monthly listing contains information on the titled sources that have been received by the British Library Lending Division. The translations included are produced by British government organizations, industry, universities and learned institutions. It also includes most doctoral theses accepted at British universities during and after 1970. Selected British official publications of a report nature, not published by HMSO, are also included as are reports and unpublished translations from the Republic of Ireland. Thus there is a wide coverage of this 'grey' or semi-published literature aimed at increasing awareness. Access is provided to over 15,000 reports, translations and theses.

Most users will begin by consulting the annual index for the relevant year. It is divided into three parts. The first section is an author index. Following each entry is such a code as: 84–09–05C–077. The first number is the year, the second is the monthly issue in which the entry will be found. The third number refers to the section within the issue and the final three digits are the item number.

Following the author index is a report number index. This enables the tracing of a report where only the number is known, but it is less likely to be of use than the other two indexes. The codes following the report identifier are the same as for the author index.

The third, and probably the most useful, index is the keyterm index. In this, keywords or compound terms derived from titles of included material are arranged alphabetically. Following each is the same format of code number referring to specific items. Selecting a key term such as GASTROINTESTINAL MUCUS gives a code number 84–11–06E–015; as before, the first numbers are the year (84), followed by the monthly issue. Find the appropriate monthly issue (November in this case) and then check the contents. This gives the page numbers corresponding to the numbered sections. The section 06 is the Biological and Medical Sciences and it can be found on page 22 within the broad area of Biological and Medical Sciences. 06E refers to Clinical Medicine. The entry has the author, institution, the number of pages, the year of publication (1983) and a bibliographic form indicator, in this case 'Thesis'.

The monthly issue has additional information, such as the contents page, which shows that material has been grouped in broad bands for retrieval. All references on a particular subject are gathered together under subject headings, and a breakdown of the entry is shown in the front of each issue. A keyterm index is included but no author index. Thus the monthly issues can be used as a current-awareness service, via the contents list.

1.8 Bibliographies

A bibliography is a list of information sources and may be produced by an individual, a library, or organizations such as publishers. The items may be ordered by author, topic or publisher. They are not restricted to print materials and can include such non-print materials as videotapes and computer programs. In the present context, bibliographies can be divided as follows:

General bibliographies
General medical bibliographies
Specialized bibliographies

Bibliographies are useful to the information seeker as they are pre-prepared book lists and can save the searcher from carrying out an individual literature search.

General bibliographies

Numerous general bibliographies are produced, and are listed in standard works such as Sheehy's *Guide to reference books*. A few selected examples are listed here:

British National Bibliography. (London: British Library, 1950–.)

American Book Publishing Record. (New York: Bowker, 1960–.)

Australian National Bibliography. (Canberra: National Library of Australia, 1961–.)

Indian Books. (Varanasi, India: Indian Bibliographic Centre, 1970–.)

Two very important listings which enable one to track down titles which are currently in print are:

British Books in Print. (London: Whitaker, 1974–)

and its American equivalent

Books in Print. (New York: Bowker, 1948–.)

General medical bibliographies

The most important general medical bibliography is:

National Library of Medicine Current Catalog. U.S. National Library of Medicine (NLM). (Washington, D.C.: U.S. Government Printing Office, 1966–.)
    This work, previously called the *National Library of Medicine catalog*, is produced bi-weekly with quarterly and annual cumulations. It includes citations for works catalogued by NLM which have an imprint date of the current or two preceding years.
    The annual cumulation is in two volumes. Volume 1 is the name and title catalogue, and volume 2 is the subject catalogue. Monographs or books are separated from serials. The catalogue uses the *Anglo-American Cataloguing Rules* (2nd edition) standards of bibliographic description, NLM classification codes and MeSH subject headings, which causes the subject section to appear very like the printed *Index Medicus*, and similar problems of usage occur. The author and title sections are relatively simple to use and the high level of descriptive cataloguing means that this publication is a very useful source of information on both English- and foreign-language materials.

Health science books 1876–1982. (New York: Bowker, 1982.)
    This is an important tool which covers the U.S. medical literature. It has a useful set of indexes. There is a subject index (Library of Congress headings with associated MeSH heading). Secondly there is a MeSH/Library of Congress (LC) and LC/MeSH equivalent index, and finally there are author and title indexes. It is therefore possible to access materials by author, title, Library of Congress or MeSH headings. Despite being densely packed, the entries are clear and contain the same level of information as found in the *National Library of Medicine current catalog*.

Medical books and serials in print. 1984. (New York: Bowker, 1984.)

This book is now issued in two volumes (subject and author index), which reflects the growth of the medical literature. It covers a wide range of topics, such as medicine, nursing, nutrition, and also more peripheral subjects such as science and technology. There is a clear description at the beginning of the book on how to use it, and there are subject, author, title, serial and publisher indexes. It is a relatively straightforward source to use but the dense, small typeface makes it hard work.

Lewis's Quarterly List. (London: H. K. Lewis.)

This publication, which appears quarterly, is a commercial catalogue that lists new books and new editions. Some of these are available from Lewis's Medical, Scientific and Technical Lending Library in London.

Specialized bibliographies

Examples of specialized bibliographies covering a narrow field of knowledge include the following:

A decade of viral hepatitis. Edited by A. J. Zuckerman. (London: Elsevier/North-Holland, 1980.)

Bibliography of the distribution of disease in East Africa. By B. W. Langlands. (Makere University College, 1965.)

Such bibliographies are of particular value when carrying out a historical literature search but they are of limited use when trying to obtain up-to-date information. They can be traced using general bibliographic tools.

Other specialized bibliographies may set out to cover only a particular type of material, such as textbooks, serials or audiovisual materials. A particularly useful example is:

Medical textbook review. 6th ed. By Victor Daniels. (Cambridge: Cambridge Medical Books, 1983.)

This book is produced annually in collaboration with the Medical, Health and Welfare Libraries Group of the (British) Library Association. It contains over 2,500 synoptic reviews of medical books and is an extremely cheap source of useful information. Produced on a word processor, it is a densely packed publication divided into clearly marked subdivisions. The three main divisions are pre-clinical, clinical and others (i.e. dictionaries, atlases and books for medical librarians). The last section, printed on yellow paper, is a list of titles that may be considered standard works for medical libraries. This is an extremely useful selected list which will be of interest to many medical workers.

Finding out about new books

Slightly different sources must be used when trying to trace new titles. The first source of information is the publishers, who produce vast numbers of publicity leaflets and stock catalogues. Important secondary sources include:

Aslib Book List (London: Aslib, 1935–.) Monthly.

This is a monthly list of selected books published in the fields of science, technology, medicine and the social sciences. It is published 'as an aid to collection development in public, academic and special libraries and information units, especially in the absence of subject expertise, examination copies of new books, or more extensive reference tools'. Entries are arranged by a Universal Decimal Classification (UDC) code and therefore medical sciences is found at 61. The books are given a rating, i.e.

A   Elementary level: general readership
B   Intermediate level: university textbook
C   Advanced level: specialist readership
D   Reference book

British Book News. (London: British Council.) Monthly.

This monthly review of new books is produced by the British Council with the aid of subject specialists. It includes general articles; for example, the November 1984 issue contains 'Social gerontology' by Peter G. Coleman, which surveys this subject and provides an extremely long and useful bibliography on the subject. The main section of this periodical, however, is taken up with book reviews which are arranged in Dewey Decimal order. The medical section contains extremely detailed critical reviews of new British books, reviews sufficient to enable a librarian or medical worker to decide whether or not to purchase a particular item.

The *Aslib Book List* and *British Book News* are both generalized selection tools. Detailed information about greater numbers of medical books can be obtained from the medical periodicals literature and specialized publications such as:

British Medicine: a monthly guide. (London: British Council, 1972–.)

This useful publication includes information on new books, pamphlets, audiovisual materials, official publications, etc. The detailed entries are arranged by type of material.

1.9 Periodicals

Periodicals, also called serials or journals, are one of the most important sources of information in any rapidly changing subject. Generally they are published at regular intervals with no envisaged date of cessation. Papers in a periodical communicate information, usually about the work of their author, and are a prime method of establishing priority for a scientist's work.

The periodical as a means of disseminating information dates back to the seventeenth century. Prior to that time, scientists communicated by letter, by means of books or informally. The birth of the periodical is linked with the establishment of scientific societies. It is generally agreed that the earliest scientific periodical, called '*Journal de Sçavans*', was first published on 5 January 1665 in France. It was followed by the Royal Society's *Philosophical Transactions* on 6 March 1665, which was to be the model for the modern periodical.

The content of today's periodicals is variable. Journals may contain any of the following: research reports which will be current and may claim priority; reviews of books, papers, conferences, etc.; descriptive and informative articles, or review articles, covering a particular topic; and news, particularly in the periodicals sent as part of membership of a society or professional body. There may be lighter articles primarily for purposes of entertainment. Periodicals often rely heavily upon advertisements, and although these can be irritating, they may guarantee survival for the periodical. Occasionally there are special sections for editorials, book lists, letters and buying guides.

Commercial or industrial organizations often produce 'controlled-circulation' journals such as *PULSE* and *General Practitioner*. The defining feature of such journals is that they are circulated free of charge. They are very up to date and usually contain very readable articles. There are, unfortunately, too many of them, produced too frequently. Jenkins (1976) considered that these non-subscription journals were read by general practitioners more often than subscription journals, though subscription journals such as the *British Medical Journal* (London: British Medical Association) or the *Journal of the American Medical Association* (Chicago: AMA) are very important in 'legitimizing' the physician's decision to use a particular drug.

In studies on the influence of particular sources of information on prescribing, journals were found to be the most influential source for evaluating a new product (Strickland-Hodge, 1980).

Use of periodicals

In science, technology and medicine, the periodical is the major means by which researchers and practitioners keep themselves up to date. In general practice the average practitioner will read between three and four journals regularly (Strickland-Hodge, 1979). Some of these will be subscription journals, some will be free.

The number of periodicals available worldwide in medicine is immense: the 22nd edition of *Ulrich's International periodicals directory* (New York and London: Bowker, 1983) lists approximately 65,000 titles and at least 5,000 of them are concerned with the medical sciences. Clearly, the average worker in medicine cannot keep up with this vast amount of available material and so must rely on others to scan it, abstract the articles and add them to some form of index for easy subject retrieval. Before moving onto these indexes and abstract journals we will consider how to track down individual journals.

Tracing periodicals

Although there is no international method of tracing a specific journal to a location, there are national sources that can help. In 1982, the *British Union Catalogue of Periodicals (BUCOP)* was replaced by *Serials in the British Library*. The purpose of this microfiche location guide to periodicals is to list all titles newly acquired by the British Library in order to ensure their exploitation. Note that although publication of *BUCOP* ceased in 1982, it is the only guide to the older-established journals other than *Current serials received*. These sources, and others, will now be considered separately.

British Union catalogue of periodicals. (London: Butterworths, 1955–82.)

This is a record of the periodicals of the world from the seventeenth century. The language and country of origin were irrelevant, however; it was sufficient for it to be included if the periodical was permanently represented in British libraries. The catalogue was produced from information received from libraries throughout Britain. It aimed to guide a prospective reader to an exact location or locations where a particular journal was housed, although, of course, holdings of libraries change and it is worth checking with the identified library prior to a visit that it still carries the desired periodical. The catalogue is arranged in alphabetical order of periodical title. The *British Medical Bulletin* (Edinburgh: Churchill Livingstone), for example, has a number of location entries. All are coded, with the code explained at the beginning of the first volume. For example BP2 is mentioned, and this code refers to the Birmingham Reference Library. Use of the introductory pages of *BUCOP* is essential if the tool is to be used efficiently. The last published edition was in 1982.

World list of scientific periodicals. (London: Butterworths, 1963–76.)

This ceased publication with the 1976 edition. However, from 1974 to 1980 a 'sub list' was available, comprising scientific, medical and technical entries taken from *BUCOP* (*World list of scientific periodicals. Scientific, medical and technical entries from BUCOP. New periodical titles 1980*).

Current serials received. (Boston Spa, West Yorkshire: British Library, 1984.)

This list contains all periodicals received by the British Library Lending Division (BLLD) and believed to be current in the year of the list's publication. There are 56,000 titles listed. Titles can be borrowed from the British Library using the inter-library loan facility available at most libraries. Titles are listed alphabetically although the one or two exceptions should be studied in the 'Notes on arrangement' at the beginning of the work. This source is easy to use. The entry for the *British Medical Bulletin* has only one code, which is the exact location within BLLD.

Serials in the British Library. (London: British Library, 1984.)

As mentioned already, this source lists only *new* titles received and so is not an exact replacement for *BUCOP*. The *British Medical Bulletin* is not listed as it is an established title, and is instead listed in *Current Serials Received*. *Serials in the British Library* does not refer only to titles available at BLLD as does *Current Serials Received*.

Some twenty-two contributing libraries combine to produce the catalogue. In this respect, *Serials in the British Library* is more of a location list or 'union catalogue'. Considering as an example *Medicine in practice: general practice supplement* (Oxford: Medical Education International), it lists three locations: the British Library Science Reference Library, the University of Dublin and the National Library of Scotland, Edinburgh. A copy can be seen at any of these establishments.

Keyword index to serial titles (KIST). (Boston Spa, West Yorkshire: British Library, 1982.)

This is a listing of the British Library's (Lending Division and Science Reference) master files of serial titles. Keywords from the title are listed alphabetically followed by the full title. There are over 200,000 titles included in the list with an additional 39,000 cross-references. The list can be used to see if a particular title is available in the British Library or to verify exact titles. It can also be used to see if a journal exists with a particular keyword in its title. Suppose a searcher requires journals on, say, antibiotics. At least a partial approach to the problem is to look up the keyword 'antibiotics'. Under this heading are eight titles including *Clinical Antibiotic Selection*. Above the heading 'Antibiotic' is the word 'Antibacterial', with one title, and below is the keyword 'Antibiotica', with five listed. Other spellings such as 'Antibiotikov' are also included.

To summarize, *BUCOP* is a useful tool for locating well-established periodicals. It is always wise to check to ensure that the library cited still keeps the periodical.

Serials in the British Library lists newly acquired periodicals and can be used to locate them.

Use the *World list* to locate journals in medicine, remembering that it ceased publication in 1976. The *Keyword index to serial titles* is useful to identify exact titles of journals or to locate specific journals with a particular keyword in the title.

Guides to the periodical literature

There are some specific directories of periodicals covering the fields of medicine and dentistry. Also, the major abstracting and indexing services publish lists of the journals they take for indexing. As the three or four thousand journals these services select are said to be the most representative, in the fields they cover, they can be scanned for useful periodical titles. Examples of these are 'List of journals indexed in *Index Medicus*' published each year with the January edition of *Index Medicus* (Bethesda, Maryland: National Library of Medicine).

Other directories such as the *List of annual reviews on progress in science and technology* (2nd edition. Paris: UNESCO, 1969), list review journals in this large area. Medicine is covered by this list and should be looked at if review journals are required.

Ulrich's International periodicals directory. (New York and London: Bowker. Every 2 years.)

Probably the most useful and readily available guide to periodical titles, however, is *Ulrich's International periodicals directory*. It is published every two years (though the 1981 edition announced that publication was to be annual). *Ulrich* alternates with a separate publication listing the less frequent periodicals, called *Irregular serials and annuals* (9th edition. New York and London: Bowker, 1984). A slight change has occurred in the twenty-second 1983 edition of *Ulrich* in that it is now in two volumes, A–M and N–Z.

Ulrich is available in most libraries and is a listing of journals in print. The coverage is worldwide. Around 65,000 periodicals are covered in the directory and all major subject fields are included. In earlier editions the information on abstracting and indexing was supplied by the editors of the journals listed. Recently, however, additional information has been obtained from the holdings lists of several of the major abstracting and indexing services. This makes the entries more reliable.

The *Ulrich* list of current periodicals is in subject order, using over 500 separate subject headings under which to include the individual periodicals. If a particular periodical covers more than one specific field, it is given one main entry and under other headings it is cross-indexed to that entry.

Each entry contains a number of specific elements which are best shown by means of an example:

610 US ISSN 0028-4793
NEW ENGLAND JOURNAL OF MEDICINE.
1812. w. $30. Massachusetts Medical Society, 10

Shattuck St., Boston, MA 02115. Ed. Dr. Arnold S. Relman. adv. bk. rev. bibl. charts. illus. stat. index every 6 mos. circ. 207,000 (also avail. in microfilm from UMI; reprint service avail. from UMI) Indexed: Biol.Abstr. Chem.Abstr. I.P.A. Ind.Med. Int.Nurs.Ind. Nutr.Abstr. Psychol.Abstr. Hosp.Lit.Ind.

The elements of each entry are:

1. A Dewey Decimal Classification number.
2. The country of publication code.
3. The International Standard Serial Number, a unique identifying number for each periodical.
4. The frequency of publication.
5. The publisher's name and address.

In addition, many of the entries contain useful additional information. The maximum additional elements are:

1. Language notation
2. Year first published
3. Country of publication
4. Price
5. Corporate author
6. Special features
7. Circulation
8. Place or places in which indexed
9. Former title
10. Annotation

The specific entry can be located by means of the subject list at the beginning of the directory, where 'Medical Sciences' is listed with an appropriate page number. There are a number of indexes at the front of *Ulrich*, which need explaining if they are not to cause confusion, and there is a list of the various abbreviations used.

If you wish to find all periodicals on a particular subject use the Cross-Index to Subjects. Not only does this give a starting page for your chosen topic, it also gives a cross-index to likely relevant sections. The index contains many headings not used as main entry points. These, generally narrow, headings are guided to the nearest main heading. 'Antibiotics' is not available as a main heading; the user is directed to look in the 'Pharmacy and Pharmacology' section.

If we look up 'Medical Sciences' in the cross-index of the 22nd edition, we are given '*see also*' references to 'Biology', 'Drug Abuse and Alcoholism', 'Pharmacy and Pharmacology' and many others. The cross-index also provides a list of sub-sections within the Medical Sciences, and one or more of these might prove relevant.

If we are searching for a relevant abstract service within the Medical Sciences, the separate index entitled 'Subject Guide to Abstracting and Indexing' should be consulted.

To find specific periodicals where exact subject fields cannot be simply defined, check the Title Index, which can be found at the end of volume 2. This lists the 65,000-plus titles in alphabetical order followed by a page number and the page number of any cross-reference topics. In the twenty-second edition 'Medical Sciences' begins on page 882. Within each section, periodicals are arranged alphabetically.

Finally, as well as collecting the abstracting and indexing services together within the main subject field, *Ulrich* provides a separate alphabetical listing immediately before the full listing of periodicals in volume 1.

Suppose we wish to know which services index the *Journal of Clinical Pathology*. We look first in the Cross-Index to Subjects. An entry at 'clinical medicine' (though not pathology or clinical pathology) guides us to the general Medical Sciences section at p. 882. From there, alphabetically to J for *Journal*, we find the details required on p. 899. We can see that this journal is indexed by *Biological Abstracts*, *Chemical Abstracts*, *Current Contents*, *Excerpta Medica*, *Index Medicus* and *Nutrition Abstracts and Reviews*. If any of the abbreviations are uncommon, they are all fully explained in the section entitled Abstracting and Indexing Services.

Sometimes the Cross-Index to Subjects is of little help. If we were looking for journals on medical aspects of human sexuality, we would have to classify the general area ourselves as Medical Sciences. On the other hand the journal *Digestion* can be easily traced. The Cross-Index guides us from 'digestive system' not only to the Medical Sciences but more specifically to the Medical Sciences—Gastroenterology and gives the starting page as 955.

Irregular serials and annuals

The 9th edition of *Irregular serials and annuals* was published in 1984, the alternate year to the publication of *Ulrich's International periodicals directory*. It lists, in one volume, over 34,000 serials published throughout the world. It covers those periodicals which are issued less than twice a year or are classed as irregular. As well as periodicals, the list covers proceedings, transactions, 'advances in' series, 'progress in' series, reports, yearbooks, handbooks, annual reviews and monographic series. The organization is very similar to that of *Ulrich*, to which it is a companion. The titles of the indexes are the same as those for *Ulrich* and have the same basic purpose.

If we wish to see what is available under the heading 'Medical Sciences', we can check generally from page 651 (9th edition). It would be particularly relevant to try to see a copy of this directory as it gathers together the 'hard to find' literature which is often particularly useful. For example, take the *Home Office statistics of the misuse of drugs. United Kingdom supplementary tables* (London: Home Office). At the entry point (found under G for Great Britain) an address is given to obtain this publication.

Ulrich's Quarterly. (New York and London: Bowker. Quarterly.)

As *Ulrich* and *Irregular serials and annuals* appear in alternate years, their content can become quickly outdated. To overcome this drawback, *Ulrich's Quarterly* is published. This provides continuous, worldwide, up-to-date information between editions of the two main directories. The format and arrangement are the same as for *Ulrich* and *Irregular serials and annuals*.

Ulrich Online

As with many large data collections, printing and compilation have been simplified and improved by means of computerization. The Bowker Serials Database is the system used to print *Ulrich's International periodicals directory*, *Irregular serials and annuals* and *Ulrich's Quarterly*.

The online service not only permits access to users but also provides listings for the 63,000 publishers to correct and modify prices for each publication of a new edition. The service became available online in March 1983. On the database host DIALOG, the service is available as File 480. Every word in the title of the periodical, the subtitle and any former title will be searchable. A single search through *Ulrich's International periodicals directory* online will be equivalent to a manual search through *Irregular serials and annuals, Sources of serials: an international publisher and corporate author directory* (New York: Bowker, 1977) and *Ulrich's Quarterly* as well as the *Periodicals directory* itself. The file is updated every four to six weeks with revisions and additions. Well over 100,000 records are now available for searching.

1.10 Abstracting and indexing journals

The number of useful medical journals and the task of reading all relevant papers in any particular area of medicine is immense. The abstracting and indexing journals aim at providing a guide to the periodical literature covering many thousands of periodicals in most languages. This permits the practitioner interested in a particular field to check on all relevant articles published in a month, a year or whatever cumulation exists.

In the current edition of Morton and Godbolt's *Information sources in the medical sciences* (dealt with in section 1.1), there is a chapter entitled 'Indexes, abstracts, bibliographies and reviews', which lists and describes many useful tools. The purpose of *this* section is to look closely at five such sources: *Index Medicus, Excerpta Medica, Psychological Abstracts, Biological Abstracts* and *Current Contents*. For other, similar sources, *see* Morton and Godbolt.

Index Medicus

Index Medicus (Bethesda: National Library of Medicine) was compiled by hand from its introduction in 1879 until 1963 when a fully operational computer system permitted 'machine printing' to go ahead. The new service was called MEDLARS, which is an acronym for Medical Literature Analysis and Retrieval System. The computer tapes which produce the 'hard copy' or printed version can be searched directly. The online service is called *Medline* (MEDLARS online) and is discussed in Chapter 2, which deals with online use.

There are a number of areas in which great care is needed when using *Index Medicus*. American spelling and word use can be a problem for users in the United Kingdom, and the use of Latin, Greek *and* Anglo-Saxon word forms can cause a problem for everyone. In terms referring to organs such as KIDNEY, LUNG or HEART, these forms may be found in *Index Medicus* but so too may RENAL CIRCULATION, NEPHRECTOMY and KIDNEY DISEASES. Generally, if the term is referring directly to the organ, then use the Anglo-Saxon form. With care and experience the problem can be overcome. If you are unsure of a term, there are a number of tools which aid the use of *Index Medicus*. The first is Medical Subject Headings or Public MeSH. This lists over 16,000 terms and indicates whether a particular term is used in *Index Medicus* or whether a more acceptable term is available. A brief note is given with each term, which is expanded in Annotated MeSH, used mainly for online use. These two tools together are invaluable in searching. A compromise has been made between the specificity of terms and the size of the 'thesaurus'. At this stage it should be noted that articles within *Index Medicus* will always be indexed under the most specific terms available.

Under any particular term in MeSH will be one or more code numbers. These refer to the position of that term in a hierarchical arrangement of terms called the *Tree structures*. These will be discussed later. If, when a term is located its Tree code number is found to be followed by a plus sign, then more specific terms exist and they should be considered when searching. Following the code number there are notes which are best explained using some examples:

IMINES
D2.491+

This shows that there are more specific terms to IMINES and that they can be found in the Tree structures under code D2.491.

IMITATIVE BEHAVIOR
F1.145.510.
68

As there is no + sign, there are no more specific terms available in this case. The term became an acceptable indexing term in 1968, as indicated by the 'historical note' 68.

IMMUNIZATION, PASSIVE
E2.95.377.330   E5.478.550.520
80; was PASSIVE TRANSFER 1973–79;

First the two Tree codes show that the term has two emphases which place it in a different part of the hierarchy. The term was introduced in 1980 and before that it was PASSIVE TRANSFER. This implies that if you search back in *Index Medicus* before 1980 you must use the term PASSIVE TRANSFER. Other data such as X references, which are common in *Index Medicus*, are concerned with the cross-referencing. Their use is explained in the MeSH introduction, which should be consulted before beginning a search.

Annotated MeSH is particularly useful for online searching. It gives more information about the scope of each term and can still be useful to *Index Medicus* searchers.

Tree structures are explained at the back of MeSH and are used to find other terms that may be of use. In particular, they are used to trace more specific terms which will narrow the search, or broader terms which will widen it. Using the previous examples, IMINES was coded at D2.491. Under this term are nine more specific terms such as CARBODIIMIDES and more specifically again CME-CARBO-DIIMIDE (*Figure 1.1*). Terms are placed within the Trees according to their meaning or meanings. The Trees are arranged alphabetically and within the alphabetical breakdown, they are further broken down by a numerical code. All terms are shown in their chosen section related to other terms within that section. Some terms are only searchable online and they do not appear as search terms in *Index Medicus*; such terms are identified by an asterisk in the Tree structure. Details of meanings are given in the Introduction.

IMINES	D2.491			
CARBODIIMIDES	D2.491.203			
CME-CARBODIIMIDE*	D2.491.203.340			
DICYCLOHEXYLCARBODIIMIDE*	D2.491.203.385			
ETHYLDIMETHYLAMINOPROPYL CARBODIIMIDE*	D2.491.203.425			
IMINO ACIDS	D2.491.485	D2.241.81.	D12.125.72.	
AZETIDINECARBOXYLIC ACID*	D2.491.485.100	D2.241.81.	D3.383.82.	D12.125.72.
POLYETHYLENEIMINE·	D2.491.650	D2.455.326.	D25.720.716.	
SCHIFF BASES	D2.491.784			

Figure 1.1 Breakdown of the term IMINES in the MeSH Tree structure

Another problem encountered when using *Index Medicus* is the strange use of precoordination—in other words, linked terms such as BRAIN ABSCESS. The problem is that some are inverted, such as EMBOLISM, AIR, and there is no guidance in MeSH from AIR EMBOLISM. Permuted MeSH is useful as it breaks up all compound terms and lists them under their separate parts showing the accepted order of coordination. Under AIR are a number of terms including EMBOLISM, AIR.

There are 16,000 terms listed in MeSH. When it is realized that there are at least twice that number of chemical compounds alone, it can be seen that the compromise of specificity to size has created a problem for searchers. If searching for a specific chemical compound not listed in MeSH or Tree Structures where does the search continue? The MeSH Supplementary Chemical Record is a relatively new addition to the range of tools, having become available in 1983. It lists 25,000 chemicals and, among other information given, it gives the heading under which that chemical has been indexed in *Index Medicus*. This information is under the (HM) Heading Mapped Section and it is where the searcher should look to find any printed information on that compound.

Index Medicus appears monthly with an annual cumulation. The arrangement of the two types of *Index* is slightly different. In the *Cumulated Index Medicus* MeSH forms the front of the first part and is followed by the Tree Structure. The second part has three sections: first, a list of journals and monographs indexed; secondly, a bibliography of medical reviews; and finally, the first part of the list of authors (other parts throughout the year have author indexes also). The most useful for the general search is the bibliography of medical reviews, which lists, under MeSH headings, well-documented surveys of the literature. All articles are indexed in parts 7 to 14 of the annual cumulation (referred to as book 7 to book 14). They are listed under the appropriate subject heading. If there are a large number of citations it will be useful to consider familiarizing yourself with the subheadings used. They are explained in the front of Annotated MeSH. They break up the references into smaller, more specific subsections of any MeSH heading and can aid searching by allowing the searcher to ignore irrelevant articles. Any non-English-language article is indicated by the use of square brackets around the title of the citation. If an English abstract is given, this is shown as ENG.ABSTR. in parentheses. The language of the article is then shown as an abbreviation. In *Index Medicus* only one author is cited at an entry. If the author's name is followed by *et al.*, then other authors collaborated in the work.

To help searchers find the full list there are a number of author indexes within the year's cumulated volume, which list authors and all coauthors in alphabetical order.

In the monthly *Index Medicus*, MeSH comprises the first part of the January issue. This first issue has as a separate section a full list of the journals indexed. In each monthly part, the reviews are at the beginning, while the final section of each monthly part is the *Index Medicus* Author Section, which again lists all authors with their coauthors.

Index Medicus has been available for over one hundred years, but there are still problems for the searcher. Try looking up NAPPY RASH—you won't find a guide from the letter N. The term required is DIAPER RASH. However, by using all the tools and taking note of the arrangement of the index, a great deal of very useful information can be accessed *much* more rapidly than would be possible using the original journals.

Excerpta Medica

Excerpta Medica (Amsterdam: Excerpta Medica) is published by Elsevier in the Netherlands and was first produced in 1946. The purpose of its foundation was to 'further the progress of medical knowledge by disseminating medical information in English'. With MEDLARS the articles are abstracted by specialized indexers using the tools mentioned previously. With *Excerpta Medica* however, indexing is carried out by physicians using an online thesaurus called MALIMET. The 'hard-copy', printed version differs markedly from that of *Index Medicus* in that it is printed as forty-four separate abstract journals, each covering one aspect of medicine, plus two drug-related literature indexes. Each abstract journal is known as a section and is numbered. Each section is built up of issues published during the year. Abstracts are provided with each entry.

There is wide subject coverage including of course human medicine but also aspects of chemistry, sociology, management and economics where they relate to medicine. Areas such as the environment and pollution control are also covered, and drugs and toxicology are very important areas to *Excerpta Medica*. Nursing and veterinary science are excluded.

About 3,500 biomedical journals are covered completely by assignment editors. Some 1,500 additional journals in chemistry, sociology management are also covered. All journals are included in the published *List of journals abstracted*. An estimated 20,000 scientific publications per year are screened with cooperation from other institutions. Over 95 percent of the abstracts come from journal articles, with only 5 percent coming from annuals, books and monographs. Some dissertations are covered but no patents.

Each of the forty-four sections of *Excerpta Medica* covers a particular subject area. The abstracts in each section are arranged according to a detailed classification scheme, a copy of which is given at the beginning of each section issue. The combined classification schemes from each section are known as

Excerpta Medica Classification or EMCLAS and consist of 6,500 polyhierarchically linked categories covering the medical literature.

Terms used to compile the subject index are of two types: Class A and Class B terms. Class A represents the major descriptors or concepts, Class B the less important terms. *Excerpta Medica* publishes a *Guide to the classification and indexing system* which covers the classification system and includes a subject index of about 5,000 terms. This means that broad terms may be found but specific terms will often be lost. Searching the printed versions is not usually a problem because of the depth of indexing and the rotation of terms. However, it is important to find the section under which your particular search term may be best searched. This can be done either by looking at the list of abstract journal titles which appears on the inside back cover flap, or by looking up a broad term encompassing the search term under consideration in the *Guide*'s subject index. This will provide a series of numbers to the right of the selected search terms. Those in bold print represent the most important sections, to be checked first. The *Guide* is particularly useful for online searching.

The problems of using *Excerpta Medica* are similar to those of *Index Medicus*. The language and spelling are American. Anglo-Saxon, Greek and Latin terminology are used and it is sometimes difficult to find the appropriate section in which to search. There is, however, no 'term inversion', as natural word order is preferred. So whereas in MeSH coordinated terms are sometimes inverted, for example EMBOLISM, AIR, this does not happen in *Excerpta Medica*.

In the cumulated end-of-year volume is a subject index. This is arranged alphabetically using major descriptors or class A terms. For each term, there is a list of all abstracts which have this as a major descriptor. The term itself is printed bold-face and is followed by the other major descriptors, minor descriptors, tags and the abstract number. If there are other abstracts of relevance they are listed in a similiar manner, though the lead-in term is replaced by a dash. The abstract numbers run from 1, which is abstract 1 in issue 1, to the end of the final issue of the year. The abstracts are first arranged in the hierarchical classification system and are then numbered, in order that they can be found easily. Individual issues of each section also have a subject index that refers to that issue only. Both cumulated and individual issues have an author index which lists all authors up to a maximum of three.

Biological Abstracts

Biological Abstracts (Philadelphia: BIOSIS) is the major abstracting service in the biological sciences. Its scope is wider than its name suggests since it also covers medicine, dentistry and veterinary science. It is published monthly with semi-annual cumulative indexes.

Biological Abstracts can be used in two ways: to browse; and to search. The abstracts are arranged under broad subject headings and by selecting the appropriate heading from the list at the beginning of each volume one can turn to the appropriate section and browse. For example, if the searcher picks up the December 1984 issue and is looking for items on paediatrics then the section heading list contains the heading 'Pediatrics' (note the U.S. spelling) and entries under the heading are found on page 9,666. At this page, there is a note stating 'Pediatric studies relevant to other subject headings will be found under those headings', which means that it is necessary to search under a series of headings in order to pick up all relevant entries. Beneath this note, there are five detailed abstracts of new research reports. Subject headings which contain many entries, for example 'Neoplasms and neoplastic agents', are divided into subsections such as biochemistry, blood and reticuloendothelial neoplasms, which makes browsing easier. There are also general cross-references at the beginning of the sections.

Detailed searching of *Biological Abstracts* involves using the indexes. The Author Index is a straightforward alphabetical listing of author names and abstract reference numbers. The format is shown below:

```
                          Personal name
AYLES Z         29811
CARSONS J N     23330        Reference number
CHEM SOC (ENGL) 20888
                          Corporate name
```

At the beginning of the Author Index, there is a useful summary of the criteria by which names are entered (up to ten authors or coauthors are entered for each item, and family names with O', M', Mc, Mac have no space, as for example MCCLELLAN).

The Biosystematic Index contains broad taxonomic categories and it is used to find items which refer to a particular phylum, class, order or family of organisms. Before searching the index, one must look at the Biosis Taxonomic Categories and select the most appropriate heading. For example, if searching on virology the category is A 2 Viruses and this is placed near the beginning of the sequential listing. Next find the appropriate place in the index; under 'Viruses' one finds the following subheadings:

VIRUSES
Viruses—General
Bacterial Viruses
Bacterial Viruses—Unspecified
Corticoviridae
:

:

:
Animal Viruses
Animal Viruses—Unspecified
Arenaviridae
:

:

Herpesviridae
:

:

:

Select the appropriate heading, say Herpesviridae, and underneath are further subdivisions such as Allergy, Cancer Therapy, Chemotherapy, General, and here are listed the abstract reference numbers. These should be noted down and they can then be found in the abstracts listing. This index is quite time-consuming to use and it is only when the searcher turns to the abstracts that he or she can be sure that the items found will be relevant.

The Generic Index is used to find items referring to a genus and/or species name, a community name, or a hybrid form. The searching procedure for this index involves: verifying the genus–species name (consider spelling variants and alternative names) then locating the entry in its alphabetic position; note the major concept emphasis; using reference numbers, consult the abstracts. A typical entry looks like this:

Genus–species	Major concept	Ref No.
Escherichia coli	ALLERGY	35572
	↑	
	Concept heading	

At the beginning of the Generic Index there is a guide to its use which gives a detailed explanation of a range of tags that are used to give specific taxonomic information; *S, for example, signifies a new species.

The Concept Index is used to find items relating to broad subject areas. To search this index, first look at the Subject Guide and select the subjects appropriate for your search. Select the appropriate Concept Heading(s) and Subheading(s) and locate these headings in the alphabetic position. Obtain the reference numbers and then locate the abstracts. In practice, the Concept Headings and Subheadings are so broad that they do not facilitate a specific manual search. For example, under the subject heading 'Medical and Clinical Microbiology—Bacteriology' of the July–December 1981 semiannual cumulative index there are more than 1,000 entries and it would be necessary to check each abstract to ascertain whether or not it was relevant. This would be an extremely slow and tedious task.

The Subject Index is used to find items on the basis of specific words appearing in the author's title or added by BIOSIS. Before searching this index, select the keyword(s) to be searched and check their spelling, adjectival forms, synonyms and the BIOSIS abbreviations list (this appears at the end of the Subject Index). Locate the words in the index and consult the entries to the left and right of the keyword for additional information on the subject context. If this appears relevant, then obtain the reference number and check the abstract. The following types of entry appear:

Subject context	Keyword	Ref. No.
7 HUMAN ANTIADDICTIVE	HEROIN/THE SWEDISH METHADONE MA1	83941
NCEPHALOGRAM/AC	ABSTINENCE IN MAN 4. SLEEP W.	69705
RAWAL SYNDROME	ADDICTION DIAGNOSIS CENTRAL	77685

This index is quite usable even though the beginnings and ends of words are chopped off so that each entry will fit on one line.

When using *Biological Abstracts* it is frequently necessary to use more than one of the subject indexes described above.

Psychological Abstracts

Psychological Abstracts (Washington, D.C.: American Psychological Association) is a monthly periodical. A table of contents in each issue has sixteen major content divisions including general psychology, communication systems and personality. There is a key to the text which includes a list of abbreviations and a description of a typical journal record.

Before consideration of the cumulated and monthly issues it is important to note that there is a thesaurus of psychological terms which should be used to select the correct entry points with the abstract journal. Unlike MeSH, the thesaurus is not issued annually. Major changes and improvements are suggested by users and indexing staff, and are incorporated in new editions. The first edition was issued in 1974, the second in 1977 and the latest in 1982. This lengthy wait for updates may cause problems when attempting a search on new topics. About one-third of the terms are accompanied by scope notes which give brief definitions or statements of the term's meaning. Noun forms are the preferred entry. When the noun can be quantified, then the plural is used, whereas the singular form is used unless the term refers to processes, properties or conditions. Natural word order is preferred when a concept is represented by a compound term. There is a thirty-six-character limit on entries and so abbreviations are used. This could cause problems in alphabetization; however, the number of abbreviated terms is small and there seems little difficulty in practice.

Cross-references are employed; words such as *use* direct the user from a non-postable term to a preferred (postable) term. Non-postable terms might include synonyms, spelling differences, abbreviations and word sequences. Broader (B) and narrow terms (N) are displayed to help the searcher refine the search:

NORMS
  use TEST NORMS
HORSES
  B MAMMALS
    VERTEBRATES
DEFENSE MECHANISMS
  N DENIAL
    FANTASY
    :
    :

Related terms (R) which guide the user to possible other areas for the search are also shown. In this case the relationship is semantic or conceptual but not hierarchical, e.g.

    PHYSICAL FITNESS
      R EXERCISE
        PHYSICAL ENDURANCE

The user can ignore them in the search or choose to follow up the relationship.

As with MeSH, historical information as to when the term was first used is included. In this thesaurus, the information is provided via a superscript number next to the postable term, e.g.

    EXPERIMENT CONTROLS[73]

Following the Relationship Section of the thesaurus which has guided the user to the postable (preferred) terms and has indicated useful relationships, there is a Rotated Alphabetical Terms Section which in jargon is a KWIC (keyword in context) type index. In this, each word of a compound term is shown in alphabetical order. Take as an example GENETIC COUNSELLING. Under G the word GENETIC is printed in bold-face type followed by 'counselling' in normal print. Under C the word COUNSELLING is in bold *preceded* by the word 'genetic' in normal type. All terms are rotated, however many there are in a compound. An interesting case arises for the abbreviations previously mentioned. If a word such as ATTITUDES has been abbreviated to ATTIT in the thesaurus because of the thirty-six-character rule, then it appears in the Rotated Alphabetical Terms Section still as an abbreviation but in position as though it were spelled out fully:

Racial and Ethnic	ATTITUDES
Sensory Handicaps	(ATTIT Toward)
Sex Role	ATTITUDES

The final section of the thesaurus is the Postable Term Codes Section. Each postable term is listed in alphabetical order to facilitate rapid selection of the correct search term. This aids spelling, which is American. Again the superscript number indicates when the term was introduced into *Psychological Abstracts*. The numeric prefixes aid online searching, e.g.

    14970 DORSAL ROOTS[73]

The thesaurus is very useful and gives a great deal of helpful information, although there are not as many entry points for British spelling as there might be. Language problems such as 'hepatic' versus 'liver', 'heart' versus 'cardio' are taken care of in the Relationship section of the thesaurus.

There is also a cumulated version of *Psychological Abstracts*. This has a January to June and a July to December index. The first listing within each index is of the journals scanned regularly and abstracted selectively. Each entry gives the year when coverage began. About 1,000 journals are listed although not all contain relevant articles each year.

Following the list of journals is an author index. Only four authors are listed; if more are cited then only the first one is used, with the addition of '*et al*'. Each author is followed by the abstract number.

The remaining 900 pages are the subject index. The index acts as a guide to the user by means of *see* references from non-postable terms: thus ABLATION (*see* LESIONS). Each index term is followed by an index phrase. From the index, the searcher goes to the abstracts corresponding to the coverage of the particular index, which may be from January to June. The cumulated list of abstracts contains a table of contents. This shows the page numbers for each of the main subjects and the subsections of these subjects. As in *Excerpta Medica* the abstracts are arranged in these broad subject areas and then numbered to the end, though, as a reference may relate to more than one subject area, the indexes should be used first.

The monthly version of *Psychological Abstracts* is arranged similarly, but has a brief subject index and an author index.

The complete unit of thesaurus, indexes and abstract journals is easy to use if care with spelling and word selection is maintained.

Collections of abstracts in selected narrow areas are available from *Psychological Abstracts*. For example, *Mental retardation 1971–1980* is organized in a similar way to other issues, using only those classification sections that are relevant.

Current Contents

It takes time to produce the indexing and abstract journals. This means that the citations within these guides to the periodical literature are not completely up to date. To make a search as current as possible the journals themselves can be scanned, or another aid can be used: the weekly publication *Current Contents* (Philadelphia and Uxbridge, Middlesex: Institution for Scientific Information) reprints and binds together contents pages of journals and distributes these as rapidly as possible. Some may be two months out of date but even for these *Current Contents* is still more up to date than the indexing and abstract journals. Others of the contents lists included may be of journal issues published as little as three weeks previously. There are two of particular relevance to medicine: *Life Sciences* and *Clinical Practice*.

Current Contents is more than a listing of title pages. Each issue has a contents list and a list of journals appearing in that particular issue. As some journals do not appear weekly, not every issue of *Current Contents* will necessarily include the same journals, so this list of journals should be scanned first. Over 100 titles are included in each of the issues of *Life Sciences* and about the same number in *Clinical Practice*.

Each issue has an editorial entitled 'Current comments' which is the same in *Life Sciences* and *Clinical Practice*. Following the comment is an Institute for Scientific Information (the compilers) Press Digest which covers items of interest or controversy from various sources. These are again the same in the *Life Sciences* and *Clinical Practice* issues of *Current Contents*.

The two issues differ from this point. Some of the titles chosen are the same in the two publications but the majority of journals covered by one are not covered by the other. The full contents pages are provided and act as a very useful current-awareness service. Following the title pages is a word index, which is an alphabetical listing of significant words in every article and book title indexed in each issue of *Current Contents*. (There is a guide to the use of this index on its preceding page.) American spellings are used. The words chosen are those from the article heading and not necessarily from the *Current Contents* entry. There is no cross-referencing in the word index and care is needed in using it if all relevant references are to be traced. Latin, Greek and Anglo-Saxon terms are used, which needs consideration when searching. Following the word index are an author index and an address directory. Finally there is a Publisher's Address Directory, which includes names and addresses of all publishers included in that issue. It is a very useful tool for current awareness.

1.11 Theses

In order to locate theses, valuable as records of completed research, there are a number of sources that can be used. The two most often considered are *Index to Theses* and *Dissertation Abstracts International*.

Index to Theses. (London: Aslib.)

Index to Theses is published by Aslib and is a guide to the theses accepted for higher degrees by the universities of Great Britain and Ireland, and the Council for National Academic Awards (CNAA). It does not include those theses which are submitted in partial fulfilment of a higher degree where there is a written examination.

The *Index* comprises two parts. Both include all subjects and cover all available theses on which information has been received in the first (part 1) or second (part 2) half of the year. The timings are approximate, as part 2 is usually available around February of the following year.

In each part, there are a number of 'indexes' to guide the user to the relevant material. The author index at the end of the volume presupposes that the user is interested in a known thesis. The author's name is followed by the item number, which leads into the body of the volume where all titles are arranged numerically. Looking at POWELL, P.H. in volume 32 part 1, the item number is given as 3,317. In the body of the index, the item number can be retrieved and is found to be 'The role of lower urinary tract sensation in outflow in the male'. Additional information is provided at this position in the index, such as the fact that the thesis is for an MD and it was awarded at the University of Bristol in 1981. The note that an abstract is available on fiche may or may not be correct. Advance information is supplied to the *Index*'s editor. If the copy is not forthcoming or if the copy provided is unreadable, or otherwise not capable of being reproduced on fiche, then availability may be a problem. If the thesis was awarded to a student researching at a polytechnic, then the award would be made by the Council for National Academic Awards, in which case no mention would be made of the original institution of study.

Looking for a specific thesis via the author listing is perhaps rare, unless one is checking to see if one's own thesis has been included. It is more usual to search using the List of

Subject Headings at the beginning of the index, or the Subject Index which precedes the Author Index at the back. This latter Subject Index is compiled from specific terms found in the thesis title.

The List of Subject Headings covers the whole of knowledge. Medicine has a number of entries scattered through the list but medicine as a whole has its own entry. Using volume 32 No. 1, medicine is on page 96 and covers everything from anatomy to the history of medicine. It is given over fifteen pages of entries, which are divided into the main medical divisions. Many of these divisions have entries in the List of Subject Headings. This broad division permits access to related works, while the Subject Index is used when a specific area is required. To find the thesis by Powell mentioned earlier, then using the List of Subject Headings we must consider the term UROLOGY, which leads us to page 106. In the Subject Index, however, there are no access points. Why? When a thesis falls into an area covered adequately by the List of Subject Headings then more specific terms in the Subject Index are not included. This can be a problem if it is not carefully considered prior to searching. The opposite happens when a specific term precludes entry into the List of Subject Headings. For example, take a thesis entitled 'Studies in thyroid growth and neoplasia'. There is no entry in the List of Subject Headings for the thyroid gland—the broad heading which includes this thesis is ENDOCRINOLOGY. However, there is an entry in the Subject Index under 'thyroid' which leads us to the mentioned thesis. There can be confusion causing relevant information to be missed, so care is needed. Even with these problems, the List of Subject Headings and the Subject Index, used together, are very useful search tools.

Availability of theses in the United Kingdom

The Standing Conference of National and University Libraries (SCONUL) proposed a four-part standard for availability of theses in Britain. These were:

1. At least one copy of every thesis should be deposited in the awarding university's library.
2. Subject to the author's consent, every thesis should be available for inter-library loan.
3. Subject to the author's consent, every thesis should be available for photocopying.
4. Authors should be asked at the time of deposit to give their consent in writing to points 2 and 3.

This standard gives borrowers the ability to obtain copies of relevant theses. The British Library Lending Division (BLLD) has, since 1971, invited universities to loan a copy of a doctoral thesis for microfilming. These copies are announced in the British Library's *British Reports, Translations and Theses* and duplicate films can be obtained from BLLD on receipt of the usual request form. Purchase of the copies of the film can usually be arranged from BLLD other than for theses from Durham or Cambridge. It is an understanding that borrowed theses can be read only on the borrowing library's premises.

Some universities place restrictions on the borrowing or copying of theses. These restrictions to the previously mentioned standard are included in the introductory pages of *Index to Theses*. For example, Cambridge, while agreeing to the deposit of at least one copy in its university library (point 1), does not, without express permission from the author, permit copying. Also, reading of the thesis should be carried out at the library at which the thesis was deposited. Other specific restrictions or comments are spelled out in *Index to Theses*.

Dissertation Abstracts International (DAI). (Ann Arbor, Michigan: University Microfilms International.)

Dissertation Abstracts International appears in three sections. A covers the Humanities and Social Sciences, B is Science and Engineering and C is European Abstracts. For medicine section B is the most relevant. This is issued monthly with an annual cumulation.

The cumulated author index is in the back of the final part of the *Abstracts*. There is no contents page so this index has to be searched for. When it is found, there is an introduction discussing the various indexes. A breakdown of the sections follows this introduction and, as this does not appear in the various cumulations, it should be looked at first. Medicine appears in various sections such as 111B Health and environmental sciences, and VB Psychology. Two pages of information about the entries follows and this includes a discussion of how non-Roman script is dealt with. The institutions, the majority from the United States, which have cooperated to produce *Dissertation Abstracts International* are listed. Then comes, not the keyword index cumulated, but an author index. Since 1977 keyword indexes appear only with the individual monthly parts and are not cumulated. This is a problem, as the abstracts themselves are useful but, in the cumulation, are difficult to trace.

The cumulated *Abstracts* has no composite contents page and can be difficult to use. (One method is to identify the required broad section, such as VB, and try to find a useful contents page within the body of the cumulation.) For this reason, the monthly parts of *Dissertation Abstracts International* are more useful, although if libraries remove the monthly keyword index then the abstracts are largely lost.

The monthly issues of *Dissertation Abstracts International* have introductory pages that are the same as for those at the front of the cumulated author index. A full table of contents is provided with an indication of the page on which relevant abstracts are printed. The abstracts are arranged in a number of sections, each of which has its own contents page. Following the abstracts is the keyword title page with a keyword followed by a title and bibliographic details. Finally a page number is given which directs the user not to an exact abstract but to the page on which it is printed. Each entry has an abstract about a quarter of a page long, which is very helpful in deciding whether or not a thesis may be appropriate.

Given a cumulated keyword index and at very least, full contents pages for each cumulated volume, this could be a useful source. At present its usefulness as a source for retrospective study is limited.

1.12 Research in progress

Sources which record research that is currently in progress are useful for the contacts they can provide. When moving into a new area of research, an already established researcher is a useful starting point. There are a number of collections of ongoing research. For the United Kingdom the following is the most useful.

Research in British universities, polytechnics and colleges (Boston Spa, West Yorkshire: British Library)

The title expresses its brief, which is to cover as wide an area of research as possible. In 1985 the title will change to *Current Research in Britain*.

The 1984 edition is divided into three volumes: Volume 1 covers the *Physical sciences*, volume 2 the *Biological sciences* and volume 3 the *Social sciences*. A fourth volume covering the humanities will be published soon. Any of these may be of interest to the worker in medicine and careful consideration as to the most relevant volume should be given. In this section we shall look only at volume 2, *Biological sciences*.

Volume 2 includes coverage in the dental sciences, medicine, obstetrics, pathology and surgery. In all there are twenty-six sections. Research within a particular subject area can be found, or research at a particular institution can be traced instead. There is a keyword index for more specific subject searching, and a list of the universities, polytechnics and colleges and their departments.

The general organization of the work is as an index arranged by subject and within subject, by institution. Broadly, a search on PATHOLOGY would begin in the List of Subject Groups at the front, where 'Pathology' is listed as Subject Code S. At the top of each page is a lettered subject code; S can be traced easily and all current research on pathology found.

If you are about to move on to a new area of research (say, gland pathology), it would be possible to trace researchers by looking through thirteen or so pages in subject code S. More effectively, you could use the section 3 index of volume 2, constructed from keywords supplied by the researchers themselves (although synonyms have been edited). There is no cross-referencing and so care is needed to check all appropriate keywords. Under ADRENAL GLANDS in the index are a number of more specific terms including PATHOLOGY, which has a subject code (previously identified as S) with a number which is an institution code for easy identification. Following the institution's numeric code is a specific entry number. If there is more than one subject code, more than one institution carrying out research, or more than one researcher in the same institution working in the area, appropriate codes and numbers indicate this in the keyword index.

These two sections of *Research in British universities, polytechnics and colleges* are the most useful when tracing someone to contact. If, however, a researcher is known in a specific field, and you wish to trace the institution at which he or she is working, use Section 2, the Name Index. The codes in this section are the same as those in 'section 3' as explained above. Looking up any known name provides the subject code or codes, the institution and the specific project codes.

The degree of detail within each entry varies. Collection of the data is based on the voluntary cooperation of participating institutions, and this means that the entry contains information provided by individuals. There can, therefore, be gaps, and in some cases projects are listed merely when it is *hoped* that work on them will soon begin. Nevertheless, the provision of a contact person is particularly useful when research is beginning or where a discussion might be useful to overcome a problem. A typical entry contains the name of the researcher, a very brief description of the research, the grant-awarding body if any, and the time allotted for the work.

References

Davinson, D. E. *The periodicals collection*. London: André Deutsch, 1978.

Jenkins, P. (1976). 'Cuts in promotional expenditure would be censorship.' *Pharmaceutical Journal* **217** (5894), 427.

Strickland-Hodge, B. (1979). 'The impact of drug information on the prescribing of drugs.' Ph.D. thesis, Birmingham: University of Aston.

Strickland-Hodge, B. (1980). 'The usage of information sources by general practitioners.' *Journal of the Royal Society of Medicine*, **73**, 857–62.

2 Online information retrieval

Online searching involves accessing files on a computer system. Typically, the files consist of either bibliographic or data records and are provided by a database producer such as the National Library of Medicine. The computer system is frequently what is termed a 'host system', and such hosts enable one to access many files, from a variety of sources, on the same computer. The host system is accessed via the telephone system. If it is located in a different country to one's own, it is necessary to use international telecommunications networks.

Online systems are typically made up of four components:

> information sources
> computer hardware
> telecommunications systems
> computer software

In carrying out an online search it is important to have a basic understanding of these components.

2.1 Online information systems

Online systems have developed from the application of information technology to the production of printed abstracting and indexing journals. This development took place in the early 1970s and has been described by Houghton and Convey (1984) and Henry *et al.* (1980). It can be summed up in *Figure 2.1*. It is important to understand how online database systems are constructed as this knowledge facilitates efficient searching of these important sources.

Database producers such as the National Library of Medicine or BIOSIS obtain source materials relevant to the database's subject coverage. These materials may include journals, books, reports, conference proceedings and patents. The source materials are then indexed and abstracted by the database producers using their own standards and procedures. The result of this process is a record; the structure of such records varies, each database producer having its own standard arrangement, as will be seen from the individual discussions of particular databases. *Figures 2.2* and *2.3* show typical records.

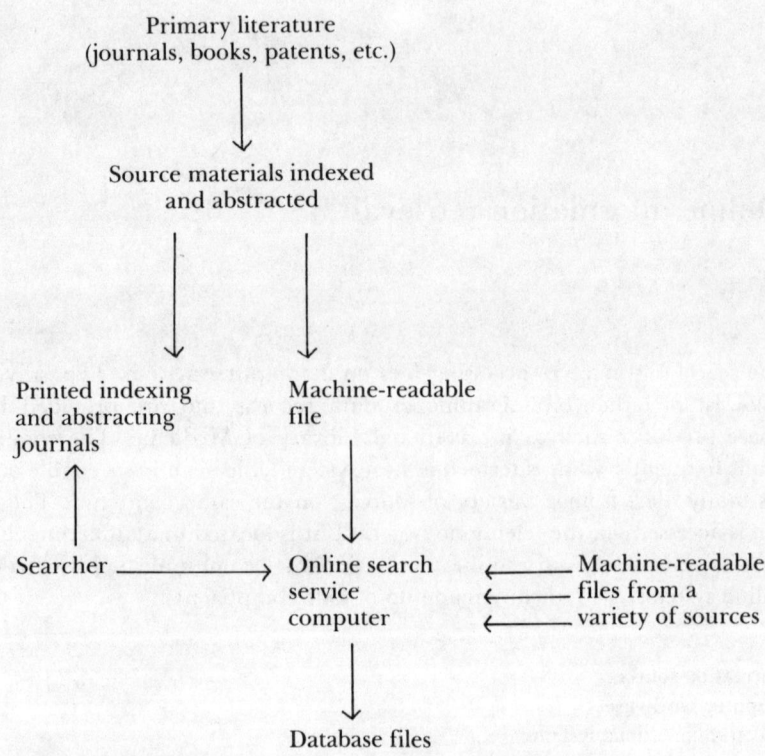

Figure 2.1 The provision of hard-copy and online services

```
1442811    84282811
Herpes viruses and the human race.
Beierle JW
CDA J (UNITED STATES) Jun 1984. 12 (6) p 27-31. ISSN 0091-4231 Journal Code: CRA
Languages: ENGLISH
Journal Announcement: 8412
Subfile: Dental ↑
Tags: Human
  Descriptors: Cytomegalic Inclusion Disease—Physiopathology (PP); Herpes Genitalis—Physio-
pathology (PP); Herpes Zoster—Physiopathology (PP); Herpesvirus Infections—Classification (CL);
*Herpesvirus Infections—Physiopathology (PP); Mutation; Stomatitis, Herpetic—Physiopathology
(PP)
```

Figure 2.2 A typical record from *Medline*

Each record is made up of a series of *fields*, such as for author and for title; and each field has a field name, such as AUTHOR. The records are normally translated into a machine-readable file, which may be used either to produce printed indexing and abstracting journals or input into an online search service computer. The latter option is what we are concerned with here.

The usual kind of file in which records are stored is a *sequential* file (one in which one record comes after another), and such files are frequently kept in

78004265
INVESTIGATION ON HERPES VIRUS OF TREE-SHREWS 1. STUDIES OF VIRAL ISOLATION BIOLOGICAL CHARACTERISTICS AND SEROLOGY.
WU X: TANG E: ET AL
INST. MED. BIOLOGY, CHINESE ACAD. MED. SCI., KUNMING.
CHIN J MICROBIOL IMMUNOL (BEIJING) 3 (1). 1983. 33–36. CODEN: ZWMZD
Language: CHINESE
Herpesvirus strains (28) were isolated from the lung, kidney and liver specimens and pharyngeal and anal swabs of tree shrews. They were identified by biological characteristics and light microscopy and EM. Tree shrew herpesvirus (THV) were of only 1 serotype. No relationship existed between THV and human herpes simplex virus. The isolation rates of THV and neutralizing serum antibody were 29.4 and 32.5%, respectively, for > 2 wk after capture. THV existed in the tree shrew in nature and in the laboratory.
Descriptors: HUMAN HERPES SIMPLEX VIRUS LUNG KIDNEY LIVER NEUTRALIZING ANTIBODY
Concept Codes: MICROSCOPY-CYTOLOG,CYTOCHEM TECH (01054); ELECTRON MICROSCOPY (01058); ECOLOGY-ANIMAL (*07508); BIOCHEM STUD-PROTEINS, PEPTIDES,-AMINO ACD(10064); BIOCHEM STUD-CARBOHYDR.(10068); METABOLISM-CARBOHYDRATES (13004); METABOLISM-PROTNS, PEPTDS,AM ACDS(13012); DIGESTIVE SYST-PATHOLOGY (14006): BLOOD/BODY FLDS-BLOOD,LYMPH STUD(15002); URIN SYST/EXT SECR-PATHOLOGY(15506); RESPIRATORY SYST-PATHOLOGY(16006); VIROLOGY-ANIMAL HOST VIRUSES(*33506); IMMUNOL/IMMUNOCHEM-BACT,VIR,FUNG(*34504); MED/CLIN MICROBIOL-VIROLOGY(*36006)
Biosystematic Codes: HERPETOVIRIDAE(02220); HOMINIDAE(86215); TUPAIIDAE(86245)

Figure 2.3 A typical record from *BIOSIS*

accession number order, new records being added at the end. An example of a sequential file is given in section 6.3. Searching a sequential file is a very time-consuming process, so additional files (indexes or dictionaries) are created to speed up this operation.

An *indexed* or *inverted* file contains a list of subject (or author) terms with the record numbers of items containing the terms. This type of file is found in such online systems as *Medline* or DIALOG, which are relatively fast to search. In the following example, the indexed file consists of:

Record numbers	Inverted File index
7, 9	Deafness
2	Menière's disease
9, 2, 4	Otitis media
3, 6	Otosclerosis

The *dictionary* file shown below contains relationships between the subject terms and their number of postings or hits in records.

Dictionary file	Number of Postings	Record numbers
Deafness	2	7, 9
Menière's disease	1	2
Otitis media	3	9, 2, 4
Otosclerosis	2	3, 6

Indexed and dictionary files are searched by the computer system, a much faster process than searching a sequential file. Every time a new record is added to a database a file of this kind will be updated. The actual method by which new index terms are entered into the indexes varies from system to system. There are three main methods of updating a file.

1. Every term in the record may be automatically indexed. A STOP list may be utilized to prevent common words such as 'and' or 'they' from being entered into the file.
2. Only terms that have been tagged by the indexer may be entered into the index.
3. Only terms that are present in a GO list, for example a classification scheme or thesaurus, may be entered into the index.
4. A combination of these methods may be used on different parts of a record. For example, a system may apply (a) to the author field, (b) to a title field, or (c) to the abstract field.

A dictionary file can normally be displayed on the visual display unit. There are two types of dictionary file. The first type, a specialized dictionary, contains postings from one particular source; for example, an author dictionary contains entries from the author field only:

Term	Postings
Allen, Neil	2
Allen, P. S.	6
Allen, W.	4
Anderson, A.	3
Anderson, Jane F.	1
Anderson, Jane K.	14

A mixed dictionary file, the second type, contains different types of entries, for instance both name and subject terms, and may indicate the source (that is, the field name) of the entry:

Term		Postings
Allen, Neil	(AU)	2
Allen, P. S.	(AU)	6
Allen, W.	(AU)	4
Anaesthesia	(AB)	400
Anaesthesia	(TI)	230
Anaesthetic	(AB)	421
Anaesthetic	(TI)	180
Anaesthetics	(AB)	408

The actual structure and method of processing records, files and indexes vary from system to system, depending upon the computer software used by individual host suppliers and database producers. From a searching point of view, it is important to note that these differences do exist and it is worth becoming familiar with the individual systems which one will use.

Sequential and indexed files will be discussed in Chapter 6.

2.2 Computer hardware

The hardware used in online searching is illustrated in *Figure 2.4*. It includes a computer terminal, a printer, a telephone and modem, the host computer and a telecommunications network.

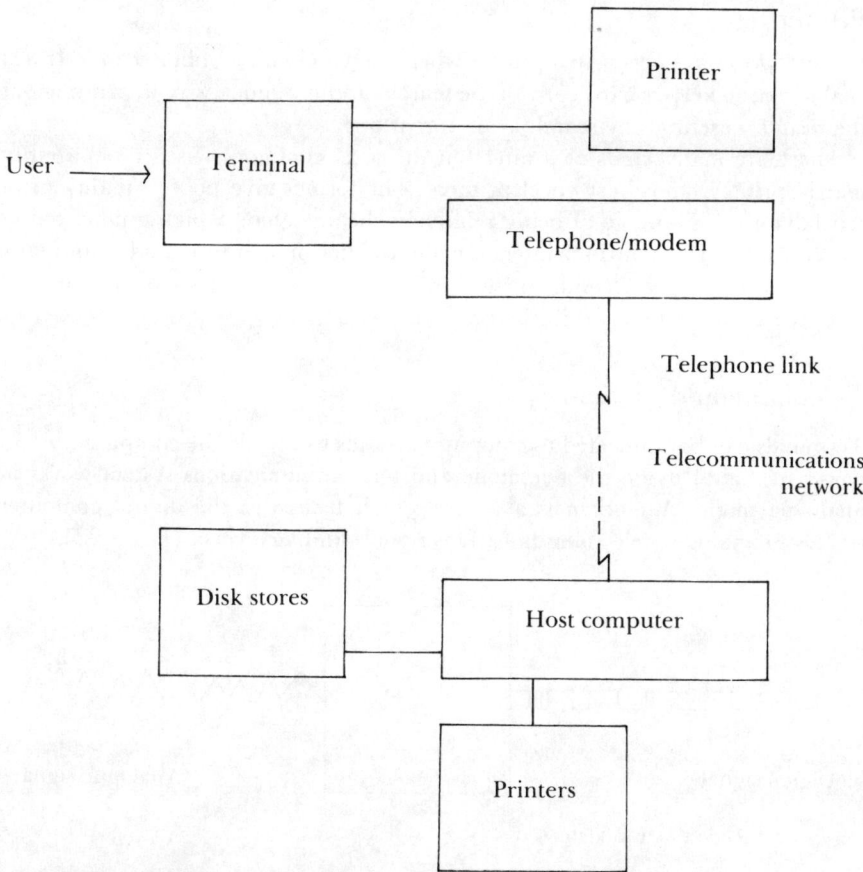

Figure 2.4 Hardware used in online searching

Terminal

There are four main kinds of terminal:

1. A keyboard combined with visual display unit (VDU).
2. A teletypewriter, i.e. combined keyboard and printer.
3. An intelligent terminal, i.e. a keyboard combined with a VDU with some processing power and memory.
4. A microcomputer consisting of a keyboard, VDU, central processing unit and external storage units.

54 Medical information: a profile

Up-to-date information on different types of terminal and their relative advantages and disadvantages can be obtained from journals such as *Online* and *Program*, and organizations such as UKOLUG (United Kingdom Online User Group) and the UK On-line Information Centre.

Printer

It is useful to have access to a printer when carrying out an online search. It will enable you to keep a hard copy of the search, and is a quick way to printing out the results—useful if the search is an urgent one.

There are many kinds of printer but the most commonly used types are dot matrix printers and daisywheel printers. The former give poorer-quality print but have the advantage of being relatively cheaper than a high-quality daisywheel printer. Dot matrix printers are also quieter in operation and print many more characters per second. Further information on printers can be obtained from the sources suggested in the previous section.

Telephone and modem

Terminals can be connected to computer systems but while the computer system works in digital mode the telephone and telecommunications system works in analogue mode. A modem is a device which translates the digital computer signals to analogue telecommunications signals and vice versa (*Figure 2.5*).

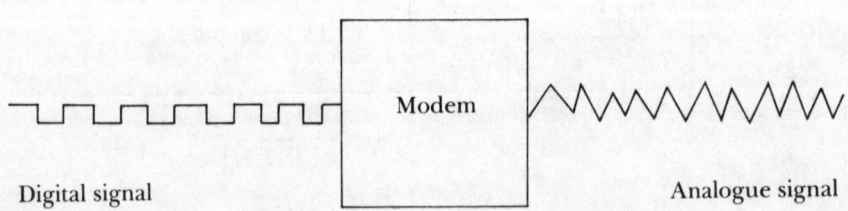

Figure 2.5 Action of a modem

There are two main kinds of modem. Hard-wired modems, the first kind, are an integral part of a special telephone set. The second kind is the acoustic coupler, a modem which contains a pair of padded cups into which is fitted the telephone handset. Unlike a hard-wired modem, an acoustic coupler does not involve an electrical connection between the telephone and the telecommunications system, and external noise may result in interference. While an acoustic coupler can be used with ordinary telephones, it cannot be used with modern trimphones and the quality of the transmitted message is dependent on the quality of the telephone handset.

The telephone line should ideally be a direct line so that one can dial direct rather than go through a switchboard, where one can be accidentally cut off. Moreover, a direct line prevents people from making internal calls, which would also interrupt or cut off transmission. As the telephone is likely to be used for long periods of time it is worth while to reserve a special phone for online use and not to publicize its number. Otherwise, normal callers may find it very frustrating if the line is engaged for long periods.

Host computer

The equipment we have discussed so far is used to access the host computer, which may be located in any of a number of countries, including the United States (DIALOG) and Switzerland (Data-Star). The host computer is normally a series of large mainframe computers and attached to these are hard disks (for the storage of files), printers (for producing outputs for searchers) and VDUs (for operating staff).

Telecommunications network

Online searching can be carried out relatively cheaply and efficiently using telecommunications networks, which are international systems designed for transmitting information to and from computers rather than between people. Important networks include Tymnet and Telenet, which began in North America but have 'nodes' in Europe and the Far East. The user can dial these nodes and so access American host systems. Euronet is an important European network.

Access to Tymnet and Telenet can be obtained via national Post, Telephone and Telegraph (PTT) authorities. In the United Kingdom, British Telecom has set up a network—the International Packet Switching Service (IPSS)—which enables searchers in the United Kingdom or United States to access each other's country's online systems. The PTT authorities charge for the use of these systems and the rate is based on connect time—the time for which the line is actually in use.

2.3 Computer software

There are two main kinds of computer software used in online searching. The host computer systems have their own software packages which determine how records, files and indexes are organized and processed within the system, and also how one can access, search and manipulate these files. The user has to learn the characteristics of individual host systems.

The second type of computer software is that used to enable an ordinary microcomputer to be used as an online terminal. These communications programs turn your microcomputer into a terminal that can 'talk' with other computers. They also enable you to manipulate information that you want either to send or to receive. These programs are discussed in more detail later in this chapter.

2.4 Searching online

The process of devising a search strategy is described in Chapter 4. Once the detailed plan has been finalized, one can start the online search. It is best to be completely prepared for the search *before* switching the terminal on. Note too that online searching is best carried out at off-peak times, when the response rate will be faster.

The process of connecting to an online system involves establishing a physical link between your terminal and the computer to be searched. If the connection is via a leased line then all you have to do is switch on the equipment—the connection is already made. If the link is via a telecommunications network then you must dial up the local node. The procedure or *protocol* is typically to:

1. Switch on the equipment (VDU, keyboard and printer) and check that the various items are correctly connected to each other. The terminal keys DUPLEX, PARITY, SPEED and LOCAL/ONLINE should be in the correct positions.
2. Dial the telephone number. Once a connection has been made you will hear a continuous high-pitched tone. If you fail to make a connection (for example, if the line is engaged, or you hear only a quiet tone), then redial.
3. Switch the signal through to the terminal either by pressing the connecting (data) button on the hard-wire modem/telephone or by placing the telephone handset into the acoustic coupler. If the former, then do *not* replace the handset into the telephone; doing so will disconnect the line.
4. Type in the terminal identifier. This enables the computer or network to identify your terminal and send information to you in a format suitable for your particular terminal.
5. To enter a particular network you will need to type in a password or passwords, and also an address. The latter will identify the system or host computer you wish to link up to.
6. To enter a particular host computer you must enter a password.

If the system doesn't respond to the password, then check the following points:

a. The shift lock on the keyboard should be off (otherwise the system will be receiving upper-case punctuation signs instead of lower-case numbers).
b. The 'online' key should be ON.
c. The 'baud' rate or 'characters per second' (CPS) switch should be selected.
d. The telephone handset, if an acoustic coupler is being used, should be placed the right way round and the connection should be unobstructed.
e. In entering addresses and passwords, has the letter O been used instead of number 0? Or letter I instead of number 1?

If the system gives double letters when addresses, passwords and commands are typed, e.g. AA112233, then check the duplex switch on the terminal and/or modem. It should be at FULL DUPLEX.

If the system responds but the user addresses, passwords or commands are not typed or displayed then check the duplex switch on the terminal and/or modem. It should be at HALF DUPLEX.

If messages such as 'DROPPED BY HOST SYSTEM' or '312 20 DISCONNECTED' appear, then the telecommunications system has failed. Start again, and when you enter the system type in a command which enables you to recapitulate on your search. On DIALOG the command required is DISPLAY SETS, which is abbreviated to DS.

A successful log-on procedure is shown in the printout reproduced as *Figure 2.6*. Once you have successfully logged on to the system you can carry out the online search.

LEE/A01-5326540029
NDIALOG
ADD?
A212300120

234212300120+COM

ENTER YOUR DIALOG PASSWORD
■ ■ ■ ■ ■ ■ LOGON File1 Fri 25jan85 5:39:45 Port06E

** FILE 61 LIMITS ARE NOT WORKING **

Figure 2.6 Log-on procedure

Using a microcomputer for online searching

Earlier in this chapter, it has been pointed out that a microcomputer can be used as an online terminal (*Figure 2.7*) if one uses the appropriate communications software.

Communications programs carry out their job by converting messages to be sent from the micro into a code such as ASCII (American Standard Code for Information Interchange) and by translating information received by the microcomputer from ASCII into a code that the microcomputer can understand. ASCII can be likened to an international language such as Esperanto and enables computers to communicate with each other.

Communications programs should be able to carry out the following functions:

1. Set the protocol, by which is meant the settings or parameters by which the two computers will communicate.
2. Create a storage space or buffer in the microcomputer's memory (RAM, random-access memory, the 'free' memory available for information storage).
3. Enable incoming and outgoing information to be stored and transmitted to and from the disks or tapes.
4. Control a printer while online.
5. Display on the screen what you are typing
6. Send and receive information to and from the modem.
7. Display received information on the VDU.

Sophisticated communications programs or additional specialized programs also enable the following to be achieved:

58   Medical information: a profile

8. Simplified log-on. Logging-on can be a very time-consuming procedure as it is necessary to type in a series of rather meaningless but very long alphanumeric strings. If you are unable to get through to the host computer then the log-on procedure must be repeated. Software packages are available which enable network and host user identifiers and passwords to be permanently stored and transmitted by pressing a few keys.

9. 'Store and forwarding' search strategy. It is very time-consuming to type in one's search strategy, particularly if mistakes are made and retyping is necessary. As online services charge by connect time, the amount of time one is online, a slow typist can boost the cost of an online search. Special software packages enable the search stategy to be typed into and stored on the microcomputer, and then forwarded to the host system.

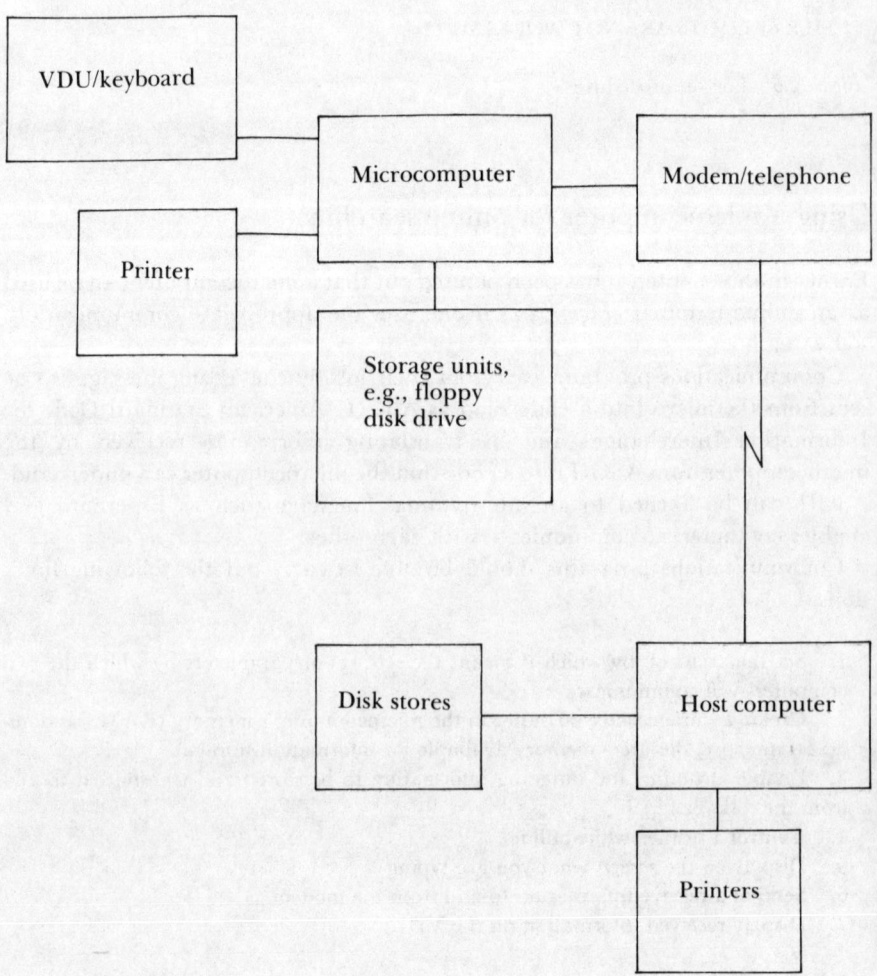

Figure 2.7   Use of a microcomputer for online searching

10. Downloading. This is the collection of data from a host computer and the storage of these data in machine-readable form, as for example on the floppy disk of a microcomputer. Burton (1984) describes the advantages of downloading as:
   a. Data can be stored at the speed they are received and thus the speed of the search is not limited by the speed of the printer. The results can be printed at leisure once the search is finished.
   b. The search results can be edited, possibly to eliminate unwanted references, to make multiple copies, or perhaps to make a more impressive-looking report.
   c. The search results can be transformed into a local information system, either on the same microcomputer or on some other local computer. Normally a reformatting program that translates the format of the downloaded data into the format of the retrieval data will be needed.
   d. Search results can be transferred from one database on the host to another, or from one host to another. For example, the results of a search for chemical compounds in a sub-structure search system could then be input to (say) a *Chemical Abstracts* bibliographic search.
   e. Retrieved data may be communicated to another computer at another location (a form of electronic mail).

One important aspect of downloading which has not been sorted out is the problem of copyright. Before downloading any data it is advisable to check with the system suppliers to make sure that you are not infringing copyright law.

11. Searching aids are becoming increasingly available for microcomputer systems. These aids include automatic storage of system commands, and command language translation, by which is meant that software translates the search strategy for one host system, say DIALOG, to the language of another, say Data-Star.

2.5 Future developments

At this stage, it is worth mentioning the development of expert systems, computer systems which are able to act as 'experts' or 'consultants'. Pollitt (1981) is working on the development of an expert online intermediary in the field of cancer therapy. His system incorporates system knowledge, subject knowledge, searching knowledge and user knowledge. The searcher need only input his or her search query in natural language and the expert system carries out the online search.

2.6 Further information

Important journals in the field of online searching include *Online*, *Online Review*, *Database* and *The Electronic Library*. Articles on this subject also appear in *Bulletin of the Medical Library Association*, *Health Libraries Review*, *Aslib Proceedings*, *Special Libraries*, *Journal of Information Science*, *Program* and *Journal of Library Automation*.

The following organizations are involved in online searching:

Online Information Centre
Aslib
26–27 Boswell Street
London WC1N 3JZ
England

Bibliographic and Information Systems Officer
Library Association
7 Ridgmount Street
London WC1E 7AE
England

UKOLUG
c/o Institute of Information Scientists
62 London Road
Reading RG1 5AS
England

2.7 Individual databases

There is a wide range of online databases relevant to medicine and allied subjects. In this section, we shall cover a range of typical sources including the most important medical databases.

BIOSIS

BioSciences Information Services (BIOSIS) provides a variety of computer-based information services.

BIOSIS Previews is the machine-readable version of citations from *Biological Abstracts* (1969–), *Biological Abstracts/RRM (Reports, Reviews, Meetings)* (1980–) and *Bioresearch Index (Biol.)* (1969–1979). *BIOSIS Previews* covers serials, books, monographs, journal articles, reports, reviews and meeting abstracts from more than 9,000 sources. Like *Biological Abstracts* it covers medicine and allied topics, and its coverage of these subjects is increasing. *BIOSIS Previews* provides information from over one hundred countries, in English. A survey of literature sources monitored for 1984 indicates the following distribution: 50 percent from Europe and the Middle East; 26 percent from North America; 15 percent from Asia and Australasia; 6 percent from South and Central America; and 3 percent from Africa.

The published *BIOSIS Search Guide/BIOSIS Previews Edition* and the machine-readable *BIOSIS Previews Authority File Tapes* provide essential information for searchers using *BIOSIS Previews*. The *Search Guide* contains five sections. The Master Index is a dictionary index containing natural-language terms from both the article's title, provided by the author, and BIOSIS's abstract, plus coded data elements (subject Concept Codes and organism names) with appropriate statistical and cross-references. These Concept Codes are a listing of approximately 600 very broad subject headings, such as 'Ecology'. Biosystematic Codes are the codes which BIOSIS allocates to higher taxonomic categories of organisms. The

Content Guide provides information on sources and records, and is also used for searching for chemical names. Finally, the Profile Guide provides information on searching *BIOSIS*.

The *BIOSIS Previews Authority File Tapes* include similar information: the BIOSIS Serial Sources Authority File, which contains a list of serials and also a list of publishers; the Subject Guide Tape, which includes concept names, synonyms and other related entries and their appropriate Concept Code numbers; the Concept Headings Tape, which contains each five-digit Concept Code number and its heading; the Organism Names Tape, which contains organisms' names and their appropriate Biosystematic Code numbers; the Biosystematic Headings Tape, which contains each five-digit Biosystematic (taxonomic) Code number and its category name; and the Master Index Authority File, which is equivalent to the Master Index described above.

When searching *BIOSIS Previews* it is worth spending a fair amount of time selecting the appropriate search terms using the above aids. BIOSIS is continually improving its search facilities to aid use of this database. For example, in 1985 it is adding thirty-two new drug affiliations to make a total of seventy-eight controlled keywords, and it is also adding four controlled terms to its vocabulary to cover drug interactions and thereby enable drug–drug, food–drug, drug–alcohol and drug–nutrient interactions to be specified at the indexing stage.

BIOSIS provides a number of additional computer services:

CLASS (*Current Literature Alerting Search Service*) is an SDI service. Users can input their search profile, with the help of BIOSIS staff if necessary, and this is run on the current *BIOSIS* database four times a month.

BIOSIS Standard Profiles (BSP) is a monthly current-awareness service. Profiles are available on twenty-eight research topics which include the following: cardiovascular bioengineering; computer cytological diagnosis; development defects—drugs; development defects—viral; human behavioural genetics; human cyclic behaviour; immunosuppressive drugs; legal aspects of addiction; medical aspects of athletic activity; physiological effects of sound; venereal disease; and viral hepatitis.

BIOSIS Information Transfer System (B-I-T-S) is a current-awareness and/or retrospective service which provides a convenient means for the computerized creation and maintenance of personal reference files. Each month subscribers receive disks or tapes containing database records selected according to a search profile. These records (which are available on tape or disk, for mainframe, mini- or microcomputer) are available in three different format options and may be edited to fit the user's requirements.

Clinical Notes On-line

Clinical Notes On-line (CNOL) is a new online service which is implemented by Elsevier-IRCS Ltd. and became available on Data-Star during early 1985. The main idea behind *CNOL* is that it will enable doctors to input and have access to case notes online. *CNOL* works in the following way:

62   Medical information: a profile

1. Clinicians, whether in hospital or general practice, submit concise notes of their observations on significant cases as they arise.
2. The *CNOL* editorial panel reviews submitted notes to ensure that presentation is satisfactory and that there is a clear contribution to knowledge.
3. *CNOL* then add an appropriate classification to the report and it appears in the *CNOL* database within an average of four weeks.
4. Authors of accepted notes receive fifty typeset and printed reprints of their notes for personal distribution.

Clinicians throughout the world can access the notes.

Presentation of the clinical notes is in the following format:

Title
Author name(s)
Address
Patient—age, sex, occupation. No details should be given which would identify the patient.
Summary—the primary symptoms observed.
History—the relevant medical history for the previous two years including details of any previous drug therapy.
Diagnosis
Case Notes—a complete description of the case. Only one reference is permitted. Full details of drugs administered to the patient.
Conclusion

To this Case Note the *CNOL* editorial board add classification details, pointers to related cases which are already present in the *CNOL* databases, and comments received from readers of the notes.

DHSS-DATA

DHSS-DATA is the online database of the Department of Health and Social Security (DHSS) Library in London. The database covers the following aspects of health care in detail:

Health Service planning and administration (for Britain's National Health Service)
Design, construction and equipment of Health Service buildings
Nursing and primary health care
Social policy
Social services administration and social problems
All aspects of the personal social services for children, families, the elderly and handicapped
Social security and occupational pensions

The following subjects are also included on the database but their coverage is not extensive:

Medical equipment and supplies
Public health and nursing

Safety of medicines
Computers
Law and technology

The database consists of records of books, pamphlets, reports, journal articles, administrative circulars and other official publications. Many of the records contain a brief abstract. An important feature of the database is the inclusion of full details, including sources of supply of official DHSS publications such as reports, discussion documents, statistics and circulars. Also included are citations of fugitive items such as pamphlets and reports from small publishers and action groups. As *DHSS-DATA* provides details of where these items may be obtained, too, it is a very good source for finding items which are otherwise difficult to track down.

One of the main disadvantages of this database is that it is relatively new (it contains records created only from late 1983) and its coverage is relatively small. However, there are plans to add to it the files of *Current Literature on Health Services* (1977–), *Hospital Abstracts* (1961–) and *Social Services Abstracts* (1977–), and also other DHSS records, such as the DHSS publications list. When these additions have been made it will become a very important information source.

Records on *DHSS-DATA* can be searched in the normal way, by using thesaurus terms from the DHSS library thesaurus, textwords from the title or abstract, personal or corporate author, or date. *DHSS-DATA* is available from Scicon.

EMBASE (Excerpta Medica Online)

The Excerpta Medica database is known as *EMBASE*. About 250,000 records are added annually, about 100,000 of which refer to drug-related information. About 30 percent of the material is available only online, not in the printed form. Although some hosts such as BRS have only one file for *EMBASE* others, such as DIALOG, have four. The first two files on DIALOG are closed and the other two are current. This use of two current files permits very fast dissemination of data.

Each article may be indexed by the staff of up to four sections of *Excerpta Medica* for inclusion in each. The time taken for the indexing to be completed by all sections will be in the region of twenty weeks. However, if the section who first index the article put these in-process data onto a file, then very current data are available even though the indexing is not complete. Data-Star uses weekly updates in its EMED file, bringing the in-process data together with the fully indexed information.

As with *Medline* (*see* later), searching techniques depend very much on the host being used, although all hosts offer certain special facilities such as online sorting of references or selective dissemination of information. The companies concerned should be contacted for further information.

The *Guide to the classification and indexing system* can be particularly useful when formulating search strategies for online use. Codes prepared from the classification scheme can be used. The way these codes are formulated for searching depends again on the host. To take a simple example, by looking in the Subject Index a section number is found. This leads the searcher to the page entitled Excerpta Medica Classification System (EMCLAS). Let us assume we have been guided to section 4 and have found the relevant chapter as 6 with subdivision (called a paragraph) as 1. We have a composite classification code of 4.6.1, which represents general subjects related to mycology. To prepare this code for searching on DIALOG, the section code needs three digits, so zeros are added to give 004. The chapter code needs two digits, so again a zero is needed to give 06. Finally the paragraph code needs two digits, giving a complete code of 0040601. The total length of the code should be eleven digits and the extras can be shown either as zeros at the end of the code or a truncation symbol can be used. Truncation symbols are systems-specific; for example, Data-Star uses the symbol # and DIALOG uses a question mark.

Martindale Online

Martindale Online is the online version of *Martindale: the extra pharmacopoeia* and it has the advantage over the printed version of being updated more regularly. As a result of its flexible structure, it is easier to find the answers to very specific questions with *Martindale Online* than with the original version. The sort of questions one might ask are such things as What drugs can cause aplastic anaemia? What narcotic analgesics are available in France?

The structure of the databank is similar to that of the book and each drug entry is broken down into records: an introduction or *class record*, which describes a particular group of drugs; drug definition and description record; a text record; an abstract record; and a preparation record. The databank also includes the date on which the record was entered or updated on the system.

Searching *Martindale Online* can be carried out in two main ways: by use of natural language (i.e. free-text searching) or by controlled language (i.e. using the *Martindale Online Thesaurus*). Natural-language searching should be used for questions on drug identity, molecular formula, tradename or other precisely defined data, whereas the *Martindale Online Thesaurus* (currently available only in printed format but soon to go online) enables one to select the appropriate terms for searching the database. The thesaurus is in two sections: an alphabetical index and a classified index. The former can be used to lead into the appropriate section of the classified index, where the search information is to be found.

The classified section is divided into the following categories: drugs, pharmaceutics, drug administration, drug absorption and fate, pharmacological actions and uses, organisms, anatomy, physiology, diseases and symptoms, medical procedures and equipment, environment and technology, and sociology. The arrangement within each section is hierarchical and cross-references indicate synonyms, related index terms and alternative hierarchies. A special set of descriptors called qualifiers can be used to define the function or context of other descriptors. For example, the qualifiers 'adverse effects', 'absorption and fate' and 'precautions' could all be used to specify the context of search on a particular pharmaceutical preparation.

Medical research directory

The *Medical research directory*, which is available in printed format as described in section 1.4, is now available online as a full-text database. It can be searched by any part of the text including institution, individual researcher, funding authority or project description.

Medline (MEDLARS Online)

The system developed to search the *Index Medicus* computer tapes was called MEDLARS. However, when it became possible to search the computer databases 'live' the system was rechristened *Medline*. The subject coverage is the same as that of the printed version of *Index Medicus*; however, there are some differences in searching techniques which should be noted.

The printed index uses *Index Medicus* IM major descriptors as entry points to the references. Usually about three of these will be chosen for each indexed article. However, the indexer will assign many more headings to the article than this, and these are searchable online. The reason why the number of subject headings in *Index Medicus* is restricted is to keep its size within reasonable proportions. Any more headings would naturally increase that size. The descriptors which are searchable online but are not printed are called minor descriptors and are identifiable in public MeSH by the small size of the print and the terms '*see under*', whereas in annotated MeSH, which should be used when searching online, only non-acceptable search terms (i.e. entry points) are shown in small print. In the Tree Structures an asterisk next to a term indicates that it is a minor descriptor searchable online but not available as a print heading. Annotated MeSH contains additional information useful for searchers, particularly the historical notes, which were mentioned in the appropriate part of section 1.10. One interesting addition on *Medline*, as compared with the hard-copy equivalent, is the inclusion of abstracts in over 60 percent of the records added since 1975.

Searching depends very much on the host. Some permit searching of recent references separately. For example, DIALOG has three *Medline* files: 152, 153 and 154. The first two are closed files covering the years 1966–1974 and 1975–1979. Between them they contain 3,000,000 records. The current file 154 covers 1980 to the present, with monthly additions of about 20,000 records. If a full search is required all files need to be searched. Other hosts have one file only. An example is Data-Star. Here the MEDL file can be searched, but there is a problem when only current references are required as an extra stage needs to be organized. Searching online, as has been mentioned, costs money and it will take longer to search the full database. (Remember too that different hosts charge different amounts. It is worth checking the current rates of charging for different databases and hosts.)

When searching *Index Medicus*, single concepts are searched with some coordination, possibly using subheadings. Complex searches can be carried out online by coordinating terms at the time of searching using Boolean logic. The way to proceed is to select a suitable term or terms from Annotated MeSH, so that a very specific search can be carried out. Some searches would lead to vast numbers of references being retrieved, which takes time and is inefficient. *Medline* has, therefore, carried out certain searches in advance and these are stored to permit quick retrieval. The terms which have been 'pre-exploded' are identified in Annotated MeSH by a large dot and they include such terms as ANTIBIOTICS, BACTERIA, WOUNDS AND INJURIES, etc. There are thirty-five such pre-explosions and they should be checked prior to searching. Depending on the host, the method of using the pre-explosions will differ and the host manuals should be checked first.

All terms in titles and abstracts are added to basic index files. This means that free-text searching is also possible using host-specific coding. For example, if you are searching for papers with CHLORPROMAZINE in their title only, DIALOG adds /TI as a suffix. Authors can be searched using the author index. Again on DIALOG, the author surname is prefixed with the letters Au=.

Pharmline

A specialist service of use in searching for drug information is the *Pharmline* system. This is an online and microfiche drug information service produced by Drug Information Pharmacists in the United Kingdom. It provides easily accessed, evaluated and up-to-date abstracts on all major aspects of drug use.

Eighty-five journals are selectively abstracted. Medicine, therapeutics, pharmacology, pharmaceutics, pharmacy practice are all covered by the service as is information science and certain relevant government report data. All therapeutic topics and drug use in special contexts are covered. Within this latter area are such topics as drugs in breast milk; alternative medicine (homoeopathy, etc.) is also included.

Because *Pharmline* is produced by the drug information specialists who will also use the system, the terminology, bias and the evaluated abstracts are precisely what is required. Terms to index abstracts are selected from a specifically created thesaurus reflecting the orientation towards current clinical and pharmacy practice.

Wiley Catalog/Online

The *Wiley Catalog/Online*, produced by John Wiley & Sons, Inc., is the online version of Wiley's *General Catalog*. This database contains full citations, descriptions and tables of contents for approximately 10,000 books, journals, software, databases, and other publications currently available from Wiley, including their medical lists. The database also contains approximately 20,000 records on forthcoming as well as out-of-print Wiley titles, plus referral records for former Wiley products now handled by others.

The *Wiley Catalog/Online* contains more than 30,000 records and contains items from as far back as 1940. The detailed record can be searched by numerous fields including author, title, subject headings and content.

Other Databases in Medicine

There are a number of other medical databases which can be of use. One such is *International Pharmaceutical Abstracts*, which consists of information from over 500 primary journals covering all phases on the development and use of drugs in pharmacy practice. The database was started in 1970 and has about 60,000 records. In the same subject area *Pharmaceutical News Index* has current information on pharmaceuticals, drugs and cosmetics. The data come from *Report of Drug Research, FDC Quality Control* and *Weekly Pharmacy Reports*. It has been online since 1976 with about 60,000 citations. It is less clinical than other, similar databases, concentrating more on the industry. It is, however, a very useful current-awareness service. *Ringdoc*, published by Derwent, is a very useful online service for the pharmaceutical industry. It has great depth of indexing and is said to be second only to *Excerpta Medica* in its usefulness for pharmaceutical literature searching. It is accessible only to subscribers to Derwent publications.

MEDOC (Medical Documents), supplied by the University of Utah, covers government documents in the health sciences from 1975. Another service, *MEDIC*, is supplied from Finland, its equivalent printed copy being *FINMED*.

PASCAL is the database supplied by Télésystèmes-Questel. It has a wide coverage of subjects, reflecting the coverage of the various sections of *Bulletin Signalétique*. It covers worldwide literature of all types including journals, French doctoral and masters theses, books and technological patents filed in France. It has been online since 1975 and has approximately 5,000,000 citations.

Toxline and *RPROJ* are useful toxicological databases.

It is difficult to choose specific databases in preference to others. Cost should be taken into account, as should file organization. The subject area may be the prime criterion and is a factor that should be carefully considered. Clinical pharmacology is particularly well covered in *Excerpta Medica*, as it is indexed by specialists, but some of this subject is available on *BIOSIS*. The preparation of drugs can be found on chemical databases such as *CA Search* (Chemical Abstracts) or *Ringdoc* if available. Patents can be traced on *PASCAL* or other Questel databases, and experimental models are on *BIOSIS*. Toxicology and environmental health may be traced using *Toxline*, *Pestdoc* and *Excerpta Medica*. Conferences in medicine can often be traced using *Medline*.

2.8 Videotex

Videotex is a term chosen by the Comité Consultatif International Télégraphique et Teléphonique (International Consultative Committee on Telephone and Telegraphs) (CCITT) to describe information systems which display screens full of data sequentially in a set format. This format in the United Kingdom uses colour and graphics with a maximum of 960 characters per screen. The screen can be an ordinary television screen or a computer's visual display unit.

Two forms of videotex are currently available, namely teletext (non-interactive videotex) and viewdata (interactive videotex). Both were designed for home use. The two systems can be crudely characterized using their method of transmission:

Teletext (non-interactive videotex)
Characterized by use of the television service.
U.K. example: CEEFAX, ORACLE.

Viewdata (interactive videotex)
Characterized by the need to use a telephone to access the data.
U.K. example of public viewdata: Prestel; of private viewdata: Baric.

Teletext

The system we now know as teletext was developed in the United Kingdom in the early 1970s by the British Broadcasting Corporation (BBC) and the Independent Broadcasting Authority (IBA), working independently. Both companies were searching for a method of sending data signals at the same time as the normal broadcast service but without these data being apparent to the ordinary viewer. Data for the provision of subtitles for the deaf were of prime interest. The IBA, which consists of a number of individual companies, required the facility to know from where a particular set of signals making up a programme was being sent. Both organizations were able to develop systems where the signals for these subtitle or source data could ride on the programme signal, accessible only to users with adapted sets.

Accessing data

The videotex system comprises a number of numbered pages which correspond to screens of data. These pages can be accessed using a remote-control handset consisting of the numbers 0 to 9 with some additional features to be mentioned later. The numbers corresponding to the required page on the service are pressed on the handset and when that page is detected the screen will show the text and graphics required. This basic system can be adapted by using a microcomputer to access it, and this technique will be discussed later in this section when we consider viewdata. The additional handset buttons mentioned are particularly useful in connection with the teletext service. For those who find the size of print difficult to read, there is a button to enlarge the information on the top or bottom half of the screen. There is a channel changer to move from one form of teletext to another or to change to television mode. In some of the more expensive sets, there is a thermolabile printer which can print out any screenful that is being viewed. As far as viewdata is concerned, these channel change buttons are of no use but the alphanumeric capabilities of a microcomputer do have interesting possibilities.

Teletext, as mentioned, dates from the beginning of the 1970s and eventually the idea of a full information service broadcast as part of the normal programme signal was developed. A television signal is built up of lines created by the passage of an electron across a cathode ray tube. To make a standard picture on the U.K. system requires 575 'lines'. However, the total number of lines available in the United Kingdom is 625. This leaves fifty 'spare' lines or spaces in the transmission signal. It is in these spaces that data to make up source data, subtitles and the teletext service can be provided.

The teletext services use four spare lines and are in the form of a continuous band of information being broadcast over and over again and transmitted as part of the normal television signal. Every set receives teletext, but only those with decoders can actually translate the signals received into pictures of text and graphics. The continuous nature of the band of data means that direct access is not possible; the user simply presses the number on the handset referring to the required page number. In the case of CEEFAX on BBC1 the index page is page 100. From this page the user can choose a page and move to it. The pages on the continuous band pass through the decoder at a rate of one page every 0.25 seconds. Although this sounds relatively rapid, it does mean that 100 pages take up to 25 seconds to pass through the decoder. As there is the same chance that the page required has just passed through the decoder as there is that it is just about to pass through it, the actual average time to wait for a page to be displayed on the screen is about 12.5 seconds, assuming that there are 100 pages in the system. If the number of pages is increased, the access time increases. If the number of lines used by the system is increased, then the time to access a page is decreased.

Information on teletext

With its small number of accessible pages (around 100 pages on each of the four services), only a small number of pages can be devoted to medical matters. The teletext service is for home use and therefore the type of information available is basic and short: first aid, diets, etc. However, it can be useful to the householder if it gives tips on what to do if one of the children is running a high temperature, and may thereby save visits to the doctor.

The medical practitioner as well as other professional people may find the financial information useful. The *Financial Times* index is updated every hour, giving an up-to-date view of the money market. Information on various shares is also updated hourly.

Cost

A capital, non-recurrent charge is made to access data on the teletext system. This covers the cost of the decoder. If the set is rented, then the cost of the decoder will be reflected in the rental. No additional charge is made to use teletext.

Viewdata

In the United Kingdom, the term 'viewdata' may be used to describe the system of interactive videotex generally but it turned out not to be possible to use the term as a trademark for the U.K. system specifically. In the United Kingdom the system available is called Prestel and has, at present, a capacity in excess of 200,000 pages.

Viewdata is defined as an interactive system for the transmission of text or graphical illustrations, stored in databanks, via the telephone or data network for reproduction on domestic television receivers or display terminals.

Development

The history of viewdata stems from the mid 1970s when Sam Fedida, working at what was then part of the (British) Post Office (now British Telecom), designed a system to give the man in the street access to a computer-based information service. The system was launched as 'Prestel for the People' though its relevance in this sector has since been questioned. The information is accessed directly; no continuous band of information is transmitted and thus a much larger databank can be provided and accessed. The user, it was anticipated, would press keypad buttons which would eventually lead him or her to the desired information.

The menu system of indexing

In a menu-driven index, the user is faced with a series of choices—menus. Choosing particular routes leads him or her nearer and nearer to the required information. To divide Prestel's 200,000-plus pages into chunks which can be conveniently numbered can lead to time-wasting and, as will be seen, time on Prestel costs money.

To illustrate the menu system, consider a search for holidays on the west coast of France. The system would first give you a basic index. From this you would select the subject index. This would show the twenty-six letters of the alphabet, each with a numeric code. Pressing the number representing H (for holidays) would lead you to a menu of H's dividing into Ha–Hecl; Hef–Hex; Ho–Hol, etc. Select the numeric code representing Ho–Hol; eventually you will find a page for holidays. The world would now be divided up and you would select holidays in Europe. From Europe select France, then move on to the relevant area of France, and so on. It is obvious that searching using menus can be time-consuming. For this reason, printed indexes have been produced, although the use of these indexes goes against the basic Prestel philosophy.

In medicine, there is a very useful printed guide called *Medipage* which is provided by the Bureau of Medical Practitioner Affairs. This guide lists, in subject and information provider order, the various medical pages available for access. To access a known page, precede the number with an asterisk (*) and end it with a hash (#).

International systems

Following the development of videotex, both interactive and non-interactive, in the United Kingdom, many other countries developed their own systems. Some of these learnt from the British problems and introduced new developments. The German viewdata system is called BILDSCHIRMTEXT and has developed an idea called 'gateway' which will be discussed later. The Canadian system

TELIDON has improved the graphics capability of viewdata far beyond that of Prestel. CAPTAIN, the Japanese system, has tackled the problem of transmitting and displaying Japanese characters. Some systems, such as the Danish and U.S. ones, have developed a keyword searching facility. U.K. research on Picture Prestel continues and other developments to improve the system are pending.

Interactive nature of viewdata

It is with viewdata that the potential of videotex is fully realized, although it is far from fully appreciated by prospective users.

The data which make up the viewdata service are stored on a number of mainframe computers positioned around the United Kingdom. Access to these computers is by telephone line, usually by means of a local call only. Access in some parts of the country is still not via a local call, and in these cases the cost of telephone access may discourage use of the service.

Information providers

Information on the viewdata service is provided not by British Telecom or Prestel as such, but by 'information providers'. These are individuals who pay an annual subscription to British Telecom (which means that they never actually own the pages). For their subscription, which is in the region of £6,500, they receive 100 pages, a user manual and the facility of forming a closed user group. The information they make available is not edited centrally and need bear no relation to the remainder of the Prestel database. Within medicine, the information providers are reputable pharmaceutical companies, and groups such as Meditel who have a great deal of experience in the medical information field and in the use of viewdata. Other useful providers in medicine are the DHSS and the British Computer Society.

Special facilities

The large number of available pages and the direct computer linkage mean that certain facilities can be incorporated into the service.

The first of these is the closed user group (CUG). The facility by which such groups can be formed allows the 'page owner' to restrict access to parts or the whole of his portion of the databank. Sometimes he does so for financial reasons and makes the restricted data available only to those who pay a subscription. Sometimes the information can be of a sensitive nature such as in medicine where the general public should not (so it is generally believed) have access. Why some of the pages are restricted is debatable but most readers of this book are likely to be members of the medical (and allied) or information professions, to whom access should not be a problem. Much of the useful medical information is held on these restricted CUGs and the information providers who 'own' the pages should be contacted if access is required. There is usually an introductory page for each of the relevant information providers, which can be used to request access.

Interaction

The internationally accepted term for viewdata, as was stated previously, is interactive videotex. The reason for the word 'interactive' arises from Prestel's facility of allowing the user to order items from the information providers while still online, to comment on a page of information and to send data to either British Telecom or the information provider, as appropriate. In medicine, data sheets, prescribing aids, films and books can all be ordered through the system. When 'Medicine in the News' was launched on Prestel (for details see later), users were asked their views on the service. In other words, they were asked to 'interact' with the system. Further examples of interaction will be given later, particularly examples concerned with training. The information provider simply provides a pro forma page which is partially completed, and the responder is asked to fill in certain details such as number of copies required. The machine used to access viewdata, whether television set or microcomputer, is registered with British Telecom and the screen has the name and address of the registered person already typed on the pro forma. The user fills in the details and either 'sends' it or cancels by pressing an appropriate number on the handset. The information provider is able to receive the message immediately. Once he switches on his own set the message will be waiting for him.

Gateway

The capacity of teletext, as we have seen, is governed by need to keep the time taken to access the required page at an acceptable level. The capacity of a viewdata service, on the other hand, is basically the capacity of the computers on which data are stored. If links are made between the viewdata computer and other external computers, a 'gateway' is opened between the user and a limitless source of data. This Gateway service has given access to shops, banks and computer programs and its potential is enormous.

Teleshopping. This involves the user gaining access to a store's computer using the Prestel handset or an alphanumeric keyboard. The user must have an account number with the store in question, but if he has he can place an order and the goods thus ordered can be sent to him direct. Credit card charging facilities can also be incorporated.

Telebanking. Almost everything that can be done via the 'minibanks' which use the plastic card technology can be done on the Prestel telebanking service. Accounts can be checked, statements ordered and transfers organized.

Gateway in medicine. Using the access to the Baric computers biorhythms can be calculated. (Biorhythms testing is available through 'Fringe Medicine'.) More relevant is the gateway access to drug information including comparative drug costs—also available through Baric.

Picture Prestel. Since 1980 the technology for showing a VHF-quality picture alongside Prestel text has been available. The problem has been that transmission of pictures of this high quality down telephone lines is very slow. New standards which have been accepted should alleviate the problem. High-quality pictures on a screen of text could be particularly useful in medicine.

Medicine on Prestel

General medical information. Before moving on to the specific medical information available through Prestel, a brief consideration of the general medical information will show the extent of the databank.

The public have access to a large number of pages with a medical content. These include 'Healthy Living—the Five Basic Rules', the Health Education Council's 'Contraception' and 'Diet and Exercise', the Department of Health's 'Social Welfare' pages and 'Health Information for Travellers'. Many pages designed to improve health in the United Kingdom are included, such as pages giving advice on how to stop smoking. Specific groups such as the deaf, the disabled and the bereaved are also catered for.

Finding related data put out by different information providers can be a serious problem. One way of overcoming this problem is to use *Medipage*, the guide to information on Prestel mentioned previously.

Specialized information in medicine. Currency is one of the most important facets of the viewdata service. A change in the information can be made in London and be available to all users almost immediately. The *Financial Times* index, together with movements of share prices and various other city news, is updated hourly. News bulletins can be altered to reflect changes in news as the day proceeds.

Medicine too is a rapidly changing subject area and as such its practitioners need current information. This need can be met by Prestel or private viewdata, which can provide updated, current information quickly and efficiently.

There are a number of services listed in *Medipage* which might be considered as current-awareness services. One such is 'Medicine in the News'. If a drug treatment causes problems, or a new drug is launched, there may be newspaper comment before doctors and other involved professionals hear of these developments. A problem can arise if a patient, seeing some comment on a drug treatment in a newspaper, brings the newspaper cutting to the doctor and asks for comments. For this reason it is important that practitioners should be informed as rapidly as possible to enable them to allay their patients' fears, or give an appropriate response to their request for a new treatment. 'Medicine in the News' aims to scan the major daily newspapers and put any information concerning drug treatments, or medicine generally, on to the Prestel databank by lunchtime of the day of publication. The service was designed by the Medical Information Research Unit in Leeds and Meditel in West Bromwich. The data are put up by Meditel on pages sponsored by pharmaceutical companies. Information from *Radio Times* and *TV Times*, in addition to that from newspapers, is added when relevant to medicine. Programmes may be of interest to the practitioner himself or he may wish a patient to see a programme to aid his treatment.

Drug information. Company-specific information is available from, for example, Astra, Glaxo and the Wellcome Foundation (via Gateway). Poisons information is available from the Scottish Poisons Information Bureau and adverse drug reaction reporting using Prestel is also possible. Using the interactive facility, information on adverse reactions can be sent to the Committee for Safety of Medicine. Apart from the novelty, there are advantages in such an idea. There is no need to fill in a yellow card (by which British medical practitioners report adverse drug reactions), there is no need to post it and doctors receive feedback on reports they send in.

Social welfare information. The U.K. Department of Health and Social Security (DHSS) distributes many leaflets concerned with benefits. These are generally available from post offices and libraries, but leaflets become out of date, libraries may run out of them, they may be misplaced and are generally untidy. An electronic storage and retrieval system can answer some of these apparent problems. The Social Information Providers Group (SIPG) coordinates the data for distribution via Prestel. The information is updated when necessary and updates are available nationally as soon as they occur. Facts, not references, are available from Prestel and so the value of, say, widow's benefit can be found rapidly while a patient is present in the surgery, pharmacy or any other establishment which has a Prestel link.

The blind can have a Braille printout, the motor-impaired can have special hardware and the elderly can do teleshopping. Prestel's interactive capabilities mean that users can place orders for goods while they are at home or when visiting the library.

Training. Programmed learning, using multiple-choice questions where the user is guided through a series of possible answers, can be set up on Prestel very simply. The Glaxo pages have a number of such 'training' packages. The Fisons private viewdata service also has useful training aids.

Another technique is to use Prestel as a mailbox, sending gathered data and receiving responses. This has been done for training purposes, using Prestel sets available in postgraduate medical centres. The general idea is that groups of general practitioners meet to discuss clinical problems, the group being led by a clinical tutor. The six most acceptable responses are typed on to the Prestel system using an alphanumeric keyboard. Perhaps ten groups around the country will be looking at the same problem. All sixty responses are fed to a clinical group, who discuss them and select the most likely ten responses, feeding them back to the postgraduate medical centres. After a number of problems have been dealt with in an evening there is a final discussion about the clinical group's responses. General practitioners who have used the system have found it interesting and useful. Anaesthesiology is another area which has used Prestel as a data-gathering service.

There are many ways in which the videotex idea can be used to the benefit of medicine. Its up-to-dateness is particularly useful. However, the cost of using the service may need considering. If you wish to use, say, 'Medicine in the News' during working hours a number of charges are payable. First there is the outlay on equipment. If you use an adapted television there will be the cost of a decoder. The rental charges for the telephone, if used on business premises, will be quite high. There is a 'computer connect' charge, currently £0.06 per minute during office hours but free from 6 p.m. until 8 a.m. Monday to Friday and free from 1 p.m. on Saturday and all day Sunday. You must also take into account the fact that you are connected via the telephone network. This means incurring a charge, usually local, for the period during which you are connected. Some pages themselves have a charge, but only twenty percent of them; none of the Prestel medical pages currently has one.

Using the microcomputer to connect. Various companies are realizing that the medical and information professions are becoming more and more computer-orientated. With this increased awareness of computers and their applications comes the desire to own one. Buying a machine for office automation, labelling, stock control or periodicals management brings the possibility of accessing data held on external computers. To connect any of the various available microcomputers, such as the BBC or IBM PC machines, one requires software and some additional hardware. This latter has been described in detail in section 2.2.

One of the functions of the software is to inform the microcomputer which of certain required functions are represented by particular keys on its keyboard. In the case of Prestel the signs * and # are necessary. The software for the BBC microcomputer sold by Meditel is disk-based and permits the creation of a local database by copying ('downloading') pages from Prestel and storing them on a disk. Tape-based software can also be used with some microcomputers; Micronet 800 have specialized in selling the necessary equipment including acoustic couplers and software. They also sell software via the Prestel system. However, accessing Prestel via tape-based software is too slow to be likely to appeal to most medical users.

Eventually the irritations involved in accessing viewdata will be ironed out and the usefulness of the source will be fully realized. In the future there is no reason why links with *MIMS* or the *British National Formulary* (London: Pharmaceutical Society Press) could not be organized and an even more useful service created.

References

Burton, Paul F. and Petrie, Howard J. *Introducing microcomputers: a guide for librarians.* Wokingham, Berkshire: Van Nostrand Reinhold (U.K.), 1984.
Henry, W. M. *et al. Online searching: an introduction.* London: Butterworths, 1980.

Houghton, B. and Convey, J. *On-line information retrieval systems.* 2nd edition. London: Clive Bingley, 1984.

Pollitt, S. An expert system as on online search intermediary. In: *5th International Online Meeting, London, 8–10 December 1981.* Oxford: Learned Information.

Tedd, Lucy. *An introduction to computer-based library systems.* 2nd edition. Chichester: John Wiley, 1984.

3 Organizations and people

This chapter provides a review of the various organizations that are involved in medicine and allied subjects. Frequently, organizations can provide information, often producing it themselves. The chapter also looks at sources of information on individual people who may be able to supply the answer to an enquiry.

A diverse collection of organizations are involved with medicine, and they can be divided into eight groups:

1. International organizations.
2. Health services, such as the United Kingdom's National Health Service (NHS) or the World Health Organization (WHO).
3. Government agencies, such as the (British) Medical Research Council.
4. Professional associations, an example of which is the British Medical Association (BMA).
5. Academic institutions, such as the Medical Information Research Unit at Leeds Polytechnic (MIRU).
6. Research institutes, including clinical research centres.
7. Commercial organizations, including pharmaceutical companies.
8. Voluntary organizations, like Alcoholics Anonymous.

Within each particular category, there is a wide range of organizations each with its own aims and objectives, activities, range of services and user population. One common feature of all these organizations is that they are involved in handling medical information. They may be involved in producing information as a result of original research, manipulating information as in the production of internal reports and bibliographies, and in disseminating information by, say, publishing it or by providing enquiry services and educating and training programmes.

In carrying out any information search it is often a good idea to start by contacting an appropriate organization, which may be able to provide high-quality information very rapidly. This information moreover is likely to be up to date, an especially important consideration when one is searching for information in rapidly developing fields in which the required information may not have had time to enter the published literature. Organizations are frequently able to identify workers who are active in a particular field and who may be able to provide the required information.

The organizations involved in medicine can be identified by using the various directories described in section 1.4. It is worth while to emphasize that it is frequently necessary to use a number of different directories in order to find the most appropriate organization. The following list will act as a reminder of some of the most useful.

> *Aslib directory of information sources in the United Kingdom*: volume 2, *Social sciences, medicine and the humanities*
> *Directory of British associations*
> *Directory of European scientific associations*
> *Directory of international and national medical and related societies*
> *Encyclopedia of associations*
> *Health sciences information sources*
> *Help! I need somebody. A guide to national associations for people in need*
> *Medical research directory*
> *Medical research index*
> *Research in British universities, polytechnics and colleges:* volume 2, *Biological sciences*
> *Self-help and the patient. A directory of national organizations concerned with various diseases and handicaps*
> *World of learning*
> *Yearbook of International organizations*

3.1 International organizations

The *World Health Organization* (WHO) is a specialized agency of the United Nations. WHO's objective is 'the attainment by all peoples of the highest possible level of health'. It is an inter-governmental agency and as the directing and co-ordinating body on international health it establishes and maintains contact with a variety of organizations: the United Nations; specialized agencies; government health administrations; and professional and other groups concerned with health. WHO assists governments (particularly those in developing countries) to improve the standard of health care services and has proclaimed the goal of 'Health for all by the year 2000', by which is meant the attainment of a level of health that permits a socially and economically productive life.

The activities of WHO include: research and development through a network of collaborating national laboratories; aid in the development of national health services; prevention and control of communicable diseases; promotion of environmental health; education and training of health care personnel; promotion of the development, production and wide availability of new medical technology (including pharmaceutical substances); and a substantial involvement in information interchange via international conferences, and an impressive publication programme.

WHO publishes a variety of materials. Its serial publications include: *WHO Chronicle, Bulletin of WHO, International Digest of Health Legislation,* WHO Technical Report series, WHO Monograph series, *World Health Statistics Annual, World Epidemiological Record,* and many other publications in a variety of languages. WHO also publishes a variety of directories, including: *The international pharmacopoeia, Medical schools* and *Manual of the international statistical classification of diseases, injuries and causes of death.*

Apart from WHO's publications, which represent an important information source, it has offices in Geneva (where its headquartes are sited), Alexandria, Brazzaville, Copenhagen, Manila, New Delhi and Washington D.C. that can be approached for medical information.

The *Council for International Organizations of Medical Sciences* (CIOMS) acts as a coordinating body between its members and their national institutions and also with the United Nations. It promotes international activities in the fields of biomedical and medical sciences and publishes an annual *Calendar of congresses of medical sciences*, which is a useful information source on conferences.

The members of CIOMS include organizations such as the International College of Surgeons, the World Medical Association and the World Psychiatric Association. They are all listed in *World of learning*. These organizations frequently publish journals, an example being the *International Journal of Epidemiology*, published by the International Epidemiological Association. They organize international conferences and their membership lists are a useful source of information on experts in a particular field. Important examples include:

International College of Surgeons
1516 Lake Shore Drive,
Chicago, Illinois 60610, U.S.A.

International Union against Tuberculosis
3 rue Georges Ville
75116 Paris, France

World Medical Association
28 ave. des Alpes
01210 Ferney-Voltaire, France

There are also many international medical organizations which are not members of CIOMS. Typical examples include:

International Center of Information on Antibiotics (32 blvd. de la Constitution, Liège, Belgium), which gathers information on antibiotics and strains producing them, in order to avoid duplication of research and development work.

International Cystic Fibrosis Association (202 East 44th St., New York, NY 10016, U.S.A.), which disseminates information on cystic fibrosis in those areas of the world where the disease occurs.

Pan-American Medical Association (PAMA) (745 Fifth Avenue, New York, NY 10022, U.S.A.) which aims to facilitate the interchange of medical knowledge and research among countries in the western hemisphere.

3.2 The health services

Wherever health services, whether public or private, are organized there are vast amounts of pertinent information for practitioners and researchers.

In the United Kingdom the National Health Service was created by Act of Parliament in 1946 and has twice been reorganized into its present fairly complex structure. The second reorganization, in 1974, was a major one which brought together:

a. The hospital and specialist services, previously administered by the Regional Hospital Boards, the Hospital Management Committees and Boards of Governors of undergraduate teaching hospitals;
b. The family practitioner services, previously administered by the Executive Councils;
c. The personal health service, covering services such as family planning, ambulance services, health centres, etc. which had previously been administered by the local health authorities; and
d. The school health service, previously administered by the local education authorities.

In 1982 a further reorganization removed a complete tier of NHS administration, bringing the decision-making nearer to the users of the service.

Information is held by various groups within this structure. Professionals have their own methods of accessing it.

3.3 Professional groups

In any country's health provision, various professional groups are responsible for various aspects of the provision of health. Physicians and surgeons, nurses, pharmacists, dental practitioners, ophthalmologists plus many other specialist groups are essential for the complete health care of any nation. The combined information they possess is immense, and the possibilities for information provision from this source are potentially vast. Generally speaking, however, the information possibilities far exceed the realities. Professional boundaries, lack of time and in some cases bureaucracy make it difficult for individuals to obtain specific information via professional groups.

The professional health and administrative groups are served by libraries and information units covering various specialities. The hospital service provides the employed staff with libraries covering nursing, medicine and drug information. However, the professionals employed outside the hospital service use external sources, such as medical libraries, to a much lesser extent.

Health Service personnel also have access to the pharmaceutical industry's medical information services. Telephoning is free as one can reverse the charges (call collect) and the information officers employed are only too pleased to help with queries on their particular products.

3.4 The library service

There are many excellent texts which look at medical and nursing librarianship in detail, and some are listed at the end of this section. A brief outline is given here.

We need first to consider at least four different types of librarian. The first is the university medical librarian, who is generally responsible for all aspects of information provision to students (clinical and preclinical), postgraduate research students and academic staff. Academic libraries are discussed in detail later in this chapter. Then there are the hospital medical librarians, both those in teaching hospitals, which still have a large student educational role, and those in non-teaching hospitals, which have a more day-to-day information updating role. Finally, there are the nursing librarians.

Many British teaching hospitals have excellent resource provision in their libraries, though no librarian will be completely satisfied with his or her library's resources! Generally, all the hospital staff will be catered for, including the administrative staff, who need to base their management decisions not only on sound reasoning but also on adequate information backing.

Non-teaching hospitals are not always as well staffed or financed. Even in newer large district hospitals space for the library is often limited and the library's level of use is in consequence frequently low. Since the NHS reorganization of 1974 many health authorities have formed information sections whose function is to collect and process data on which to make management decisions. It is perhaps sad to reflect that many small libraries are staffed by unqualified personnel who are expected to provide a full information service. Updating courses are arranged with these specific staff in mind with the idea of trying further to educate them in the newer developments.

The larger British nursing schools have libraries run by qualified staff, but in other hospitals nurses must use the medical library, in which stocks are often lacking in the nursing subjects.

In the United States a network has been developed to promote among other things the easy access of information. An enquirer, after trying the local hospitals, can next try resource libraries. If he meets no success here, he can contact the National Library of Medicine.

Continuing education programmes for health care librarians are a popular means of keeping their knowledge up to date both in the United Kingdom and the United States. In the former, national organizations such as the Library Association's Medical, Health and Welfare Group run a number of relevant courses and the Medical Information Research Unit at Leeds Polytechnic specializes in running courses in information handling for family doctors, pharmacists and medical librarians (qualified and unqualified).

To find a medical library in the United Kingdom, use the *Directory of medical and health care libraries in the United Kingdom and Republic of Ireland 1982* (5th edition. London: Library Association Publishing, 1982). This lists over 400 establishments and new editions appear from time to time. The *Directory of health science libraries in the United States* (2nd edition. Chicago: ALA, 1974) lists almost 3,000 medical libraries; other countries have similar publications.

The vast majority of publications mentioned in Chapter 1 will be available through almost any medical library. However, more libraries are cancelling subscriptions to expensive abstracting services in favour of their 'pay per use' online equivalent. Searches can often be carried out with the prior agreement of the medical librarian.

A final word on libraries. This book is intended for those who wish to search the literature for themselves, and no one should be discouraged from doing so.

Never forget, though, that there is an efficient information guide in the form of a librarian.

3.5 Drug Information Units

For the carrying out of a piece of specific, drug-related research, the best organization to contact is a drug information unit. In the United Kingdom these are located in hospitals, not necessarily teaching hospitals, and can be found in each of the fourteen regions of England, in Wales and in Scotland.

Although drug information has been disseminated from hospital pharmacy departments for many years, the setting up of the regional units is relatively recent. The London Hospital established one of the first units in the 1960s, and the first Regional Centre was started in Leeds in 1973.

All regions have a Regional Drug Information Unit with a specialist pharmacist. In some cases, the units are staffed by medics as well as pharmacists. Regional units have more specialized resources than local hospital units, which are therefore encouraged to liaise with the regional units. The regional units provide bulletins or drug letters, comparing products and evaluating treatments.

The objective of the drug information units is to provide advisory information to medical and allied staff in hospitals and the community, and to achieve maximum safety, efficiency and economy in drug use. Any queries on drugs, whether from hospital staff or not, can be answered by these units. It may be useful to make a note of their telephone number for future reference.

Some drug information units provide specialist services. For example, the Welsh Drug Information Unit also provides an information service on alternative forms of medicine and houses a unique collection of literature on the subject. The West Midlands Drug Information Service and Trent Regional Drug Information Unit specialize in 'drugs in breast milk' and answer all types of enquiry, give information and advice, and provide copies of papers. Further information about this and other hospital drug information units in the United Kingdom can be obtained from *DISC—Directory of hospital pharmacists engaged in information work*. The latest edition was produced by the Wessex Regional Drug Information Service in 1984.

3.6 Government bodies

Virtually all the world's governments have agencies involved in different aspects of medicine. Most of these bodies maintain their own libraries and information units and are an important source of medical information.

In the United Kingdom, their libraries are succinctly described in the *Guide to government departments and other libraries and information bureaux* (London: British Library Science Reference Library, 1984). This guide is clearly laid out and information on medicine and related topics can be found under the headings: medical sciences, psychology and psychiatry, pharmaceutical sciences, and occupational health and safety. Informative entries give the following details for each establishment address: telephone number, telex number, names and positions of staff, stock and subject coverage, availability, opening hours, services and publications. The following entry is typical:

DEPARTMENT OF HEALTH AND SOCIAL SECURITY

MAIN LIBRARY
Alexander Fleming House, Elephant and Castle, London SE1 6BY

TELEPHONE: 01-407 5522

TELEX: 883669

ENQUIRIES/LOANS: Exts 6363/6415

LIBRARIAN: J H Wormald, BSc (Econ), ALA

SENIOR LIBRARIANS: A B Cooper, MLS, ALA (Reader services/Social services information); D S Buchanan, MA, ALA (Health information services); J H Martin, ALA (Bibliographical and support services).

STOCK AND SUBJECT COVERAGE: 200,000 volumes and pamphlets on health services, public health, medicine, and the personal social services. Approx. 1,600 current periodicals indexes to periodical literature maintained.

AVAILABILITY: To staff; other libraries and health authorities in England for borrowing; research workers and other accredited persons, by appointment, for consultation of material not readily available elsewhere.

HOURS: 09.00–17.00 Monday to Friday.

SERVICES: Enquiry service; loans; bibliography compilation; current awareness and abstracting services; online information retrieval.

PUBLICATIONS: *Hospital Abstracts: a Monthly Survey of World Literature* (began January 1961); *Social Service Abstracts* (monthly, began January 1977); *Current Literature of Health Services*; *Current Literature on General Medical Practice*; *Library Bulletin* (all monthly); *Selected Abstracts on Occupational Diseases* (quarterly); bibliographies on specific topics; *Periodicals Currently Received in Headquarters Libraries* (quarterly); *Library Guide*.

Another useful source is the *Directory of British official publications*, which is compiled by Stephen Richard (2nd edition. London: Mansell, 1984) and is a directory of some 1,300 organizations. It includes information on central government bodies such as the Department of Health and Social Security and on regional bodies like the East Anglian Regional Health Authority. While this directory is chiefly concerned with the publications of the bodies it lists, it does provide addresses, phone numbers and contacts. It has useful organizations and subject indexes.

Information on government bodies in the United States can be obtained from:

Benton, Mildred
Roster of federal libraries: agency, geographic, subject
Arlington, Virginia: ERIC Document Reproduction Service

Benton, Mildred
Federal library resources: a user's guide to research collections.
New York: Science Associates/International

Washington information directory
Washington, D.C.: Congressional Quarterly

For other countries, it is frequently worth tracking down equivalent publications if one is seeking information on local aspects of health care. A useful starting point is the catalogues of government publishing houses.

3.7 Professional associations

Medical and allied subjects are served by numerous professional groups which have been established by practitioners to support their activities and needs. These associations frequently provide excellent information services.

Like international associations, national associations include both general and specialist bodies. A comprehensive listing can be found in *World guide to scientific associations and learned societies* (4th edition, edited by Barbara Verrel and Helmut Opitz. Munich: K. G. Saur, 1984). The following selective list indicates a few of the services available in various subject areas in the United Kingdom and United States.

General medicine

American Medical Association
Dearborn Street
Chicago
Illinois 60610
Founded 1846

British Medical Association
BMA House
Tavistock Square
London WC1H 9JB
Founded 1832

Institute of Medicine
2101 Constitution Avenue
Washington, DC 20418
Founded 1970

National Medical Association
1301 Pennyslvania Avenue NW
Suite 310
Washington, DC 20004
Founded 1895

Royal College of General Practitioners
14 Princes Gate
London SW7 1PU
Founded 1952

Royal Society of Medicine
Wimpole Street
London W1M 8AE
Founded 1805

Specialist medicine

American Association for the Study of Headache
5252 N. Western
Chicago
Illinois 60625

American College of Sports Medicine
PO Box 1440
Indianapolis
Indiana 46206

British Association of Sports Medicine
49 Blakes Lane
New Malden
Surrey KT3 6N3

British Migraine Association
178a High Road
Byfleet
Weybridge KT14 7ED

Allied to medicine

American Dental Association
211 E. Chicago Avenue
Chicago
Illinois 60611
Founded 1859

American Ophthalmological Society
200 SW 1 St.
Rochester
NW 55905
Founded 1864

American Pharmaceutical Association
2215 NW Constitution Avenue
Washington, DC 20037
Founded 1852

86   Medical information: a profile

British Dental Association
63–64 Wimpole Street
London W1M 8AL
Founded 1880

British Optical Association
10 Knaresborough Place
London SW5 0TG
Founded 1895

Pharmaceutical Society of Great Britain
1 Lambeth High Street
London SE1 7JN
Founded 1841

Nursing association

Royal College of Nursing
20 Cavendish Square
London W1M 0AB

The above associations are a useful starting point when contacting organizations in the United Kingdom and United States. However, the *World guide* covers over 150 countries in both subject order and country order.

3.8   Academic institutions

Universities, polytechnics and colleges which have medical or related subject departments have specialist library facilities and, frequently, specialized information units in the field. Information on these facilities can be obtained from directories such as the *Directory of medical and health care libraries*, already mentioned, which covers the United Kingdom and Ireland. Other countries have similar publications, such as the *Directory of health science libraries in the United States*. Most academic medical libraries have specialist staff who can provide useful and expert assistance.

Academic libraries' information facilities normally include a specialized reference collection (containing many of the directories mentioned earlier in this book); a textbook and monograph collection; periodicals, abstracting and indexing services; online search facilities; and audiovisual materials.

Specialist information units based in academic bodies may be self-financing or may be funded from the parent body or external organizations. For example, the Oncology Information Service (OIS), located within the Medical and Dental Library at Leeds University, is funded by the Department of Health and Social Security through the Yorkshire Regional Cancer Organization. The OIS provides clinicians in the cancer field with a series of monthly and bi-monthly current-awareness bulletins on different aspects of cancer. Each bulletin lists up-to-date references culled from the scanning of approximately 1,500 journals. There are nineteen of these bulletins covering topics such as: Breast cancer;

Cancer chemotherapy; Skin cancers; Nursing aspects; Tumour makers; and Pain relief. They are available free of charge to National Health Service workers in the Yorkshire region and are available to others by special arrangement. The OIS also provides computerized retrospective and SDI (Selective Dissemination of Information) searches, for a fee; these searches are personalized to suit the exact requirements of the enquirer concerned.

Specialist libraries or information units may be entirely funded by their parent academic body. An example of this type of organization is the Girdlestone Memorial Library, which is an Oxford University departmental library within a teaching hospital. Its subject coverage is quite specialized, being limited to orthopaedics, rehabilitation medicine and orthopaedic engineering, and its services include online searches. Details of these and other similar organizations in the United Kingdom can be found in the *Aslib directory*, and *World of learning* provides worldwide coverage of libraries and information units which are attached to academic organizations.

3.9 Research institutes

Research institutes may be part of an academic institution, or associated with a professional association, government agency, commercial organization or voluntary agency. Alternatively, they may be completely independent. Research institutes may be located via listings such as *Research centers directory: a guide to university-related and other non profit research organizations* (6th edition. Detroit, Michigan: Gale Research, 1978).

Most research institutes have some kind of library or information unit. For example, the Clinical Research Centre of the Medical Research Council in the United Kingdom houses the John Squire Medical Library (Watford Road, Harrow, Middlesex HA1 3UJ). This library is available to the staff of CRC and Northwich Park Hospital, all Medical Research Council staff and other bona fide users at the discretion of the librarian. The library stock includes 18,000 books and 660 current journals on clinical medicine and related sciences. Services provided include inter-library loans, translations and online searching, as well as a publications programme.

3.10 Commercial organizations

A variety of commercial organizations are involved in medicine: private medical organizations, pharmaceutical companies, suppliers of medical equipment and insurance companies. Many of them have specialized information departments to which enquiries can be directed, which saves the time-consuming business of having to track down the right person to deal with a query.

The major pharmaceutical companies have specialized library and information units. One example is the Boots Company plc, which has a research library based in Nottingham that is available to members of the company and to others with recommendation and/or on giving prior notification together with their reasons for wishing to use the library facilities. The library's stock includes approximately 50,000 volumes and pamphlets and 1,700 current serials covering medicine, biology, chemistry, pharmacy, pharmacology, biochemistry, food science, cosmetics and other topics. The library provides a variety of services and will answer enquiries provided that they fall within the scope of the library and do not conflict with the company's interests. It provides a variety of publications to company employees.

In the United Kingdom, pharmaceutical companies can be tracked down with the aid of organizations such as the Association of the British Pharmaceutical Industry or with the help of directories such as *Kompass*. This publication, *Kompass. United Kingdom* (East Grinstead: Kompass, 1983), provides a detailed guide to products and services (volume 1) and company information (volume 2). Pharmaceuticals fall under section 31 of the Kompass subject coding and there is a detailed listing of types of product with the name and address of the producing company. Additional details of the company can be obtained by looking in volume 2, which is split up on a geographical basis with an alphabetical index of companies.

Suppliers of medical equipment can be identified via their trade associations using appropriate directories of associations or via commercial directories such as *Kompass*. There are a few specialized information units which deal with this subject.

The Biomedical Instrumentation Advisory Service (BIAS), which is based at the Clinical Research Centre (Watford Road, Harrow, Middlesex) covers information sources, commercially available biomedical instrumentation, equipment and materials, sources of supply (over 4,000 suppliers are indexed), electronic, analytical and general laboratory apparatus, aids for the disabled, hospital equipment and laboratory and research chemicals. Its information officer will deal with enquiries but charges a fee.

The Supply Library of the Department of Health and Social Security (14 Russell Square, London WC1B 5GP) is a government library based in London and handles enquiries on medical supplies and equipment.

3.11 Voluntary organizations

A variety of voluntary organizations provide support and aid to people in need. They vary in size (from one person working at home to a group with full-time employees) and in the type of assistance that they can provide, which may be financial help, counselling, or support via a self-help group. As these organizations depend on voluntary help they are sometimes short-lived. Organizations such as the Citizens Advice Bureaux in the United Kingdom (which can be traced via the telephone directory) frequently maintain files on local and national organizations.

A few directories set out to list voluntary organizations. One of these is *Help! I need somebody. A guide to national associations for people in need*. It was compiled by Sally Knight (London: Kimpton, 1980) and covers more than 700 U.K. organizations which help people (or their relatives or friends) who have a specific medical or social problem. Entries are arranged alphabetically by the name of the organization, which is in bold type. Each entry consists of the organization's name, a contact, address, phone number and a brief description.

Another useful guide is *Self-help and the patient. A directory of national organizations concerned with various diseases and handicaps*. This booklet, now in its eighth edition and published by the Patients Association in London, lists national organizations that give information and advice to individuals (or their relations) suffering from particular diseases, physical or mental handicaps. The organizations are arranged alphabetically by name under headings such as 'Addictions', 'Deafness' and 'Sight Disabilities'.

3.12 Individuals

A very important source of information which is frequently overlooked by librarians and information scientists is individual people. Much important and up-to-date information is not available in printed formats and can only be obtained from researchers at the forefront of a particular field of knowledge.

These people can frequently be identified by papers that they have published or presented at conferences. Some abstracting and indexing services, including *Science Citation Index*, provide the names and affiliations of authors. Another means of identifying individuals involved in current research is to use publications such as *Research in British universities, polytechnics and colleges* (details are given in section 1.12).

There are many important directories which enable individual medical practitioners and research workers to be identified. Professional associations publish their own lists of members who are authorized to practise a profession. In the United Kingdom, medical practitioners are listed in the *Medical register*, which is published annually by the British Medical Association. Entries are arranged alphabetically by surname and give address, phone number, qualifications, data of qualifying, sex and, for married women, maiden name. However, the *Medical directory*, also an annual publication (London: Churchill), includes much additional information, including details of medical schools and hospitals in Britain and Ireland, and short biographies of members of the profession who are registered with the General Medical Council, giving degrees, medical school attended, current position, previous posts and professional publications.

Most countries provide equivalent publications. In the United States, the American Medical Association publishes a two-volume *American medical directory* which lists registered medical practitioners.

References

Carmel, Michael. *Medical librarianship*. London: Library Association, 1981. (Handbooks on Library Practice series.)

Darling, Louise (ed.). *Handbook of medical library practice*. 2 vols. Chicago: Medical Library Association, 1982.

4 Search strategy

In the preceding chapters we have concentrated on developing awareness to sources of information in medicine. In this section we shall concentrate on the practicalities of searching the literature by suggesting a logical strategy to ensure that any search is as complete as possible. To be comprehensive, this search strategy will cover both the manual and the online searching techniques.

4.1 Basic requirements

Equip yourself with a set of 5×3 in ($12\frac{1}{2} \times 7\frac{1}{2}$ cm) record cards and a suitable record cardbox. Using cards rather than paper permits a later rearrangement of the retrieved references prior to finding the actual articles.

Make a careful record of where you search. Include here details of editions of, for example, the indexes used. Also keep a record of the keywords with which you choose to search at each stage. We shall see later the best way of organizing data within the cardbox or within a computer database.

4.2 Getting to grips with the topic

New topics need defining. The definition gives the searcher not only a better understanding of the topic but also shows up synonyms and other possible search terms; medical dictionaries and encyclopedias are useful at this stage. Note all new keywords.

Throughout this section we shall be talking about searching generally but there are two types of search: those carried out for oneself and those carried out for someone else, perhaps a researcher.

When carrying out searches for others it is necessary to spend time at an early stage defining terms and finding out the researcher's exact needs. It is important to obtain some basic ideas before going on. Define the subject before you visit the researcher, so that you can, with confidence, use acceptable terminology. Another good idea is to make a brief summary or written report of the topic for discussion with the researcher. Use a questionnaire to obtain the basic details such as urgency (an urgent search may require an online search to be carried out immediately), the number of years which the researcher wants the search to cover, a few keywords and if possible some relevant references. In particular, ask if there is a general text available. Find out how many references the researcher thinks may be retrieved. Check whether all languages are acceptable or if there are restrictions in this respect. A basic questionnaire is shown as *Figure 4.1*.

92   Medical information: a profile

Name of searcher . . . .

Title of the proposed search . . . .

1. Is the scope of the query adequately represented by the above statement? If not please expand or restate it.
2. Please list key terms, phrases or concepts to describe the topic.
3. What are the subject areas involved in the study of the topic?
4. Why do you require a bibliography on this topic?
5. Do you wish to place a language restriction on the search?
6. What time period do you wish the bibliography to cover?
7. Approximately how many references do you think will be retrieved?
8. Do you already know some references relevant to the query? If so would you please list below three relevant references?
9. Could you recommend a general text to enable the searcher to obtain background information?
10. Please indicate the most convenient times for the searcher to contact you.

Figure 4.1 Typical questionnaire for sending to a researcher prior to conducting a search for him or her

Armed with this information use the textbook, if one was recommended, to help clarify the search topic. From this point searching for oneself and searching for others are very similar.

A literature guide is always useful. Its particular relevance comes when searching a new subject area. To find a suitable one use a directory such as *Walford* or any of those described in Chapter 1. Alternatively, many medical libraries provide literature guides to their own stock. The usefulness of literature guides should, however, be taken in conjunction with their limitations. Generally they are produced by librarians or information scientists rather than scientists, although some do have a major contribution from specialists.

If a bibliography is required, check that one has not already been produced in your subject area; directories such as *Walford* or Sheehy's *Guide to reference books* can again be used to find them. If one is available, check the date of the latest entries and bring the search up to date using the techniques suggested in the next section.

Consider a specific topic such as antibiotics. We can check by using *Walford* to see if there is a specialist encyclopedia. There is: Glasby's *Encyclopaedia of antibiotics* is cited. Also in *Walford* is Gottlieb and Shaw's *Antibiotics*, by means of which mechanisms of action and biosynthesis of antibiotics generally can be investigated. Literature guides do not usually cover such a specific area; however, Morton and Godbolt's *Information sources in the medical sciences* does give a number of useful sources in the subject.

The subject should now be understood, and general references and possibly bibliographies may have been retrieved. If this is all that you or the researcher required, end the search here. To bring your knowledge of the topic up to date, further steps need to be taken.

4.3 Use of abstracting and indexing journals

Abstracting and indexing journals have been discussed in Chapter 1, as have periodicals. In this section we shall briefly consider their use in the search.

The majority of references used in current medical practice will be in the form of periodical articles. To read the vast number of periodicals available would be an immense and inefficient task. However, the various abstracting and indexing journals available cover the majority of significant periodicals published in medicine throughout the world, and can be used to locate relevant articles.

If research has turned up a particularly relevant periodical, or if the researcher has provided one, check in *Ulrich's International periodicals directory* to see if an abstracting service or an indexing journal is mentioned as covering that periodical title. The two most commonly used medical abstracting/indexing services are *Index Medicus* and *Excerpta Medica*. These two sources, and similar ones, have been described in section 1.10; their layout and techniques for their use were discussed, as were problems associated with their use.

Using the Medical Subject Headings for *Index Medicus* (MeSH), appropriate keywords with which to search may be selected. These will of course be based largely on keywords chosen from the references found earlier. However, as we have seen, *Index Medicus* uses a controlled vocabulary and some modification will almost certainly be necessary. Subheadings break up the references within the body of *Index Medicus* and they should be used for speed.

Reviews are often a good starting point in a search and so the section on medical reviews at the beginning of the monthly issues or the separate issue of the *Cumulated Index Medicus* should be searched first using the selected keywords. Although 'antibiotics' was too narrow a subject for which to find, say, a literature guide, the term is too broad to search directly in *Index Medicus*. If the tree number is located in the back of MeSH, over 100 specific antibiotics can be traced for searching. If it is the general subject area that is required, this can be found using the term ANTIBIOTICS in the review section of most monthly editions. Many articles under various subheadings can thereby be retrieved. They will all be review articles and will thus be very useful for starting the search. The next step is to search in the *Index* itself. As was mentioned earlier, *Index Medicus* cites only one author in the Medical Reviews section or in the bibliography itself and if all authors are required one must turn to the back of the monthly edition where they are all listed alphabetically.

The method of searching in *Excerpta Medica* has been discussed in Chapter 1 and will not be discussed further here except to remind the searcher that although *Excerpta Medica* includes abstracts and therefore provides something by which to check the relevance of any cited article, it is much more out of date than an index, for the same reason.

When relevant articles have been decided upon from their citation in an indexing or abstracting journal, certain details will need recording on the record cards. The minimum needed will be the article's title, author's or authors' name(s), the source (in other words the journal in which the article was published), the volume number of that journal and its part number if shown, the page numbers and the language it is in. It will also be helpful, when requesting the article from the British Library Lending Division, if a record is made of the source by which the reference was traced (in this case, *Index Medicus* or *Excerpta Medica*). How these elements can be built up on the record card will be discussed later.

In order to consolidate the information given so far, consider a specific example using *Index Medicus* in a search for references on a particular chemical compound, in this case carbamol. The first tool to use is MeSH. No references under this heading are found and no guidance as to where to look is given. As carbamol is a chemical substance, check the MeSH Supplementary Chemical Record as described in Chapter 1. The term is in, and it is mapped to the broader term METHYLUREA COMPOUNDS. Returning to MeSH, the mapped heading METHYLUREA COMPOUNDS can be traced and relevant articles found under this heading. There is a tree number which has an added + sign, indicating that there are more specific terms on which to search. However, when the tree number is located, it turns out that the terms which are more specific are not relevant to the search in hand. The MeSH Supplementary Chemical Record entry can be used to search online, although if a free-text search is employed, then all synonyms (also shown in the supplement) must be used. When an existing reference has been located by research or from the discussions with the researcher and has been shown to be particularly relevant, *Science Citation Index* can be used. This tool can be used to bring the search forward in time and to broaden it out.

4.4 Bringing the search up to date

Having used the appropriate indexes and abstract journals it will be noticeable that many articles have come from the same few journals. At this stage it is useful to identify these core journals and locate them. It may also be found that a few key authors have been responsible for writing the majority of the relevant articles; make careful note of who these authors are. The third point that may have been noticed is that even if the most up-to-date editions of the indexes have been used, many of the articles are nevertheless several months old.

The next task, if the search is to be complete, is to bring it up to date by locating the most recent articles retrieved from the core journals. The dates of these articles are used as the starting point for a journal-by-journal updating search. Moreover, the list of key authors can now be used in, for example, the author list at the end of the monthly editions of *Index Medicus* to see if other, related references have been missed. It is worth searching other abstract journals or indexes too, using these names. To try to bring search up to date for the journals not considered to be core periodicals, use a relevant *Current Contents*.

4.5 Other sources useful in searching

The vast majority of relevant periodical articles will have now been retrieved—and, as previously indicated, research in medicine is generally recorded in periodical articles. There are, however, elements of the search which have been as yet ignored. In certain specialized searches, for example on prosthetics or new compounds of possible medical importance, patents will need to be searched. Their control is well documented and discussed in earlier sections of this work.

Another source of possible relevance is the report. Government departments and industrial sections produce reports which may, as has been already mentioned, contain negative as well as positive results. In areas such as prescribing trends, reports are very important and should be considered carefully.

The research produced from universities and polytechnics for higher degrees is recorded in the form of theses. It may be argued that these are naïve records of initial research efforts but they are often the only record and should be considered too. Using *Index to Theses* or *Dissertation Abstracts International* will enable relevant theses, whether master's or doctoral, to be retrieved.

Usually the last source to consider in a retrospective search, but the one which should be the first to be considered when starting a new subject, is the records of research in progress. These sources, as we have seen, lead searchers, researchers and interested personnel to other individuals working in a subject area. *Research in British universities, polytechnics and colleges* records their names and subject interests. Select the volume most relevant to the aspect of work you are undertaking and check the subject index.

Although online searching is merely a different way of accessing the same sources, the techniques employed are different and the next section will deal with them in detail. The manual techniques we have seen so far are summarized in *Figure 4.2*.

4.6 Online searching techniques

The hardware and software involved in online searching have been described in Chapter 2. In the remainder of this chapter we are going to concentrate on online searching techniques.

Preparing for a search

It is worth while to spend quite a lot of time—frequently, a couple of hours will be needed—in preparing for an online search. This time should be repaid by a quick, relatively cheap, successful search.

It is important to be equipped with *up-to-date* versions of the following documents: thesauri and classification schemes; searching guides; appropriate dictionaries; and handbooks. These tools can all be used to prepare a detailed search strategy.

As with the manual search described earlier in this chapter, it is necessary to get to grips with the topic. Note down the following details:

Summary of the search topic
List of keywords and their synonyms normally used to describe the topic
Details of recent relevant references, people or organizations working in this field
How comprehensive a search is required

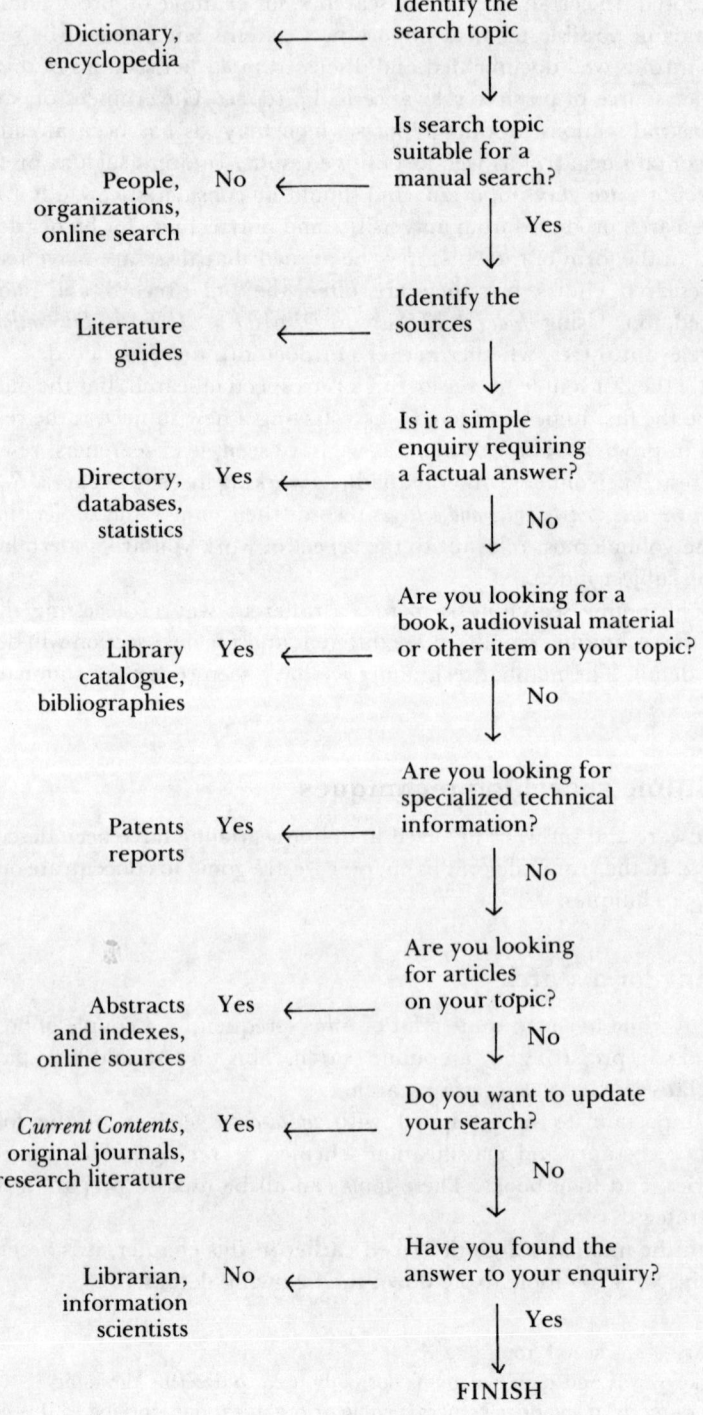

Figure 4.2 Summary of the techniques to be followed in manual searching

How many references the searcher expects
Limitations of data, language, etc.
The urgency of the search

Next, decide whether an online search is the most appropriate method of carrying out a search. The advantages of carrying out an online search include:

1. Fast access to a wide range of information sources.
2. Fast searching as compared with manual searching. A typical online search may take 15–30 minutes; the same search carried out manually could take one to two days.
3. Accurate searching. During a manual search clerical errors may be made through tiredness or carelessness and this source of error is unlikely to occur in an online search.
4. Ability to search the databases to a depth and degree of specificity which is almost impossible on manual systems. For example, it is possible to search for key terms in abstracts and to use Boolean logic to refine the search.
5. Access to extremely up-to-date information. Information in an online database tends to be available earlier than in the printed equivalent.
6. Some databases contain information which is not available in a printed version.

The disadvantages of carrying out an online search include:

1. The cost both for carrying out a particular search and the cost of obtaining and maintaining the computer hardware.
2. The need for the user to be trained in carrying out online searches.
3. The databases tend to cover only material published since the early 1970s. Online searching would therefore be useless for searching for information published in the 1950s, say.

Before deciding to carry out an online search, it is worth asking the following questions:

Will an online search provide the required information?
Is it the most appropriate source of information?
Is it a cost-effective and beneficial means of obtaining the required information?

The next step is to decide which database to search. The following parameters should be taken into account: subject coverage; journal coverage; record coverage; indexing methods; up-to-dateness; cost; and accessibility. If a comprehensive search is required then it is frequently necessary to search a whole collection of databases, such as *Medline, EMBASE, BIOSIS, Psychoabs* and *Scisearch* (i.e. online versions of *Index Medicus, Excerpta Medica, Biological Abstracts, Psychological Abstracts* and *Science Citation Index*) in order to obtain a comprehensive search.

One should then decide which host system to use from a choice of systems such as BLAISE, ESA-IRS, QUEST, Pergamon-Infoline, SDC Orbit, Euronet Diane, Data-Star, and Lockheed DIALOG. The choice of the host system will depend on the following factors:

The subjects covered by the host system. Coverage can be assessed by reading the relevant sections of the system manuals and obtaining a list of the relevant databases covered by each host system. In the medical field, BLAISE covers *Medline*, *Toxline*, *Cancerlit*, *Cancerproj*, *Clinprot*, MeSH and *RTECS* while DIALOG covers *BIOSIS Previews*, *EMBASE*, *IPA*, *Medline* and *Scisearch*.

It is important to investigate how the databases are dealt with by the host system. How far back in time do they go? Is a particular file divided up? (For example, BLAISE has six different *Medline* files.)

Can you restrict your search to particular fields, e.g. author, conference year, grant amount, language, summary language?

What devices are available to aid your search? For example, QUEST and DIALOG have a LIMIT command which enables one to limit a search by a number of parameters, DIALOG has a SORT command which enables one to sort the output according to specified commands.

What is the likely performance of the host system? Is it going to be affected by local time?

Can you have a choice of print formats: for instance, to print either the full record entry with an abstract or just the bibliographic reference?

What is the cost of the system? Some host systems have 'special offers' on searching particular databases; others have special 'training databases' which are relatively cheap to use and can be used to obtain online searching experience.

Working out your online strategy

The next step is to prepare a detailed search strategy. Ideally, the searcher should carry out an online search by typing in a prepared written search strategy. Initially, one analyses the search topic and breaks down the subject into its logical components. Unnecessary concepts can be excluded. For example:

Topic.
Articles published in English after 1983 on the treatment of herpes virus infection in young adults.

Breakdown.
Herpes virus infection.   English language.
Treatment.   1983–.
Young adults.

Then one should select the search terms, and the following tools can be used to aid this process: reference works; thesauri and classification schemes; known relevant references; printed forms of the database; and online dictionaries, thesauri and classification schemes. For example:

Herpes genitalis.   Drug therapy.
Herpes simplex.
Herpes virus infection.
Young adult.   1983–.
Adult.   English language.

Search strategy 99

The search terms should then be put into a format suitable for use in interrogating the database. This involves:

Checking to see how the system and files deal with punctuation and forms of words. Is American or British spelling used? Is an author's name represented as Smith, Derek or Smith D.?

Checking the indexing policies of the system.

Checking which fields can be searched; possible examples are descriptor field and abstract field.

Checking methods of limiting the search, for example by format, date, language.

Checking for and removing potentially highly posted, general terms such as HUMAN, RESEARCH, ACTIONS.

Checking for proximity searching, which means specifying search terms that must be close to one another on the record. For example, in the case of VISUALLY (w) HANDICAPPED, the (w) specifies in this case that the two words must be adjacent.

The search can then be planned in detail. This involves noting down:

The system commands.
The search terms.
The search strategy used to relate the search terms.

The system commands are obtained from a system manual and typically enable one to: enter a particular database or file, search it, display the results of the search on the VDU screen, print out the results of the search, then to leave the system.

The search terms will have been obtained by the procedures described above. The search strategy involves relating these subject terms through Boolean logic. There are three Boolean operators: AND, OR and NOT.

AND is used to narrow a search, e.g.

Set 1   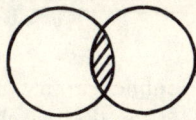   Set 2
E. coli   Enzymes

Set 1 AND Set 2 is equivalent to the shaded area and contains references on *E . coli* **and** enzymes.

OR is used to broaden a search, e.g.

Set 1   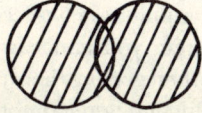   Set 3
E. coli   C. tetani

Set 1 OR Set 3 is equivalent to the shaded area and contains references on either *E. coli*, *C. tetani* **or** both.

NOT is used to exclude a topic from a search, e.g.

Set 1   Set 3
E. coli   C. tetani

Set 1 NOT Set 3 is equivalent to the shaded area. It contains references on *E. coli* but **not** *C. tetani*. Note that in this case items on *E. coli* **and** *C. tetani* are excluded from the selected set of references. The NOT operator should be used with care.

An example of the use of the AND and OR operators in shown in *Figure 4.3*.

It is important to plan what to do if the search turns out to be too broad or too narrow in terms of the number of references retrieved. If too broad, it can be made smaller by the use of the AND statement to restrict the search, possibly by language, date or experimental animal. If the search is too narrow and results in too few references then it can be broadened by the use of the OR statement. It is best to consider all the possible outcomes of the online search and draw up appropriate contingency plans.

```
? BEGIN 154
      25jan85 5:40:40 User 7243
      $0.26 0.017 Hrs File1*

File154:MEDLINE – 80–85/Jan
      Set    Items Description
? SELECT HERPES GENITALIS
      1      418 HERPES GENITALIS
? S HERPES SIMPLEX
      2     1656 HERPES SIMPLEX
? C 1 AND 2
      3       70 1 AND 2
? C 1 OR 2
      4     2004 1 OR 2
? S HERPESVIRUS INFECTIONS
      5      727 HERPESVIRUS INFECTIONS
? C 4 AND 5
      6       55 4 AND 5
```

Figure 4.3 Selecting a *Medline* file and searching it using the AND and OR logic

Searching online

Once the detailed search plan has been finalized, the online search can be started. It is important to be one hundred percent prepared for the search *before* you switch the terminal on, but to remain flexible during the actual search. Online searching, incidentally, is best carried out at off-peak times when the response rate will be faster.

The process of connecting to an online system has been described in Chapter 2. It involves connecting your terminal to a remote computer via a telecommunications network; once you are connected to the system you can carry out your search. If you are carrying out the search for another person then request that person to sit in on the search. If the search goes badly and you cannot see an easy way of producing the desired results then log-off and return to the planning stage.

The results of the search can be obtained online (an expensive option) or offline, the printout being mailed to the searcher (a cheaper option). The output can normally be produced in a variety of formats. DIALOG, for instance, has eight:

Format 1   DIALOG Accession Number
Format 2   Full Record Except Abstract
Format 3   Bibliographic Citation
Format 4   Abstract and Title
Format 5   Full Record
Format 6   Title
Format 7   Bibliographic Citation and Abstract
Format 8   Title and Indexing

Frequently, a searcher will display a few references in full format on the VDU screen and if they appear to satisfy the enquiry, have the full set of records printed offline.

Sophisticated facilities

Many online systems have a range of sophisticated facilities that can be used to facilitate efficient searching.

Index searching

In some systems, including DIALOG, it is possible to search the *indexes* of a number of databases at the same time. This enables the searcher to identify which databases contain relevant references. The search procedure involves:

1. Selecting the index database (rather than a particular database such as *Medline*).
2. Selecting the group of file indexes which you wish to search. This can be done by inserting file numbers, subject categories or both.
3. Typing in your search strategy.
4. Reading the results. This will indicate how many references on your particular topic are found in the files which you have selected at stage 2.
5. You can then enter the individual file and view the appropriate references.

An example of index searching is shown in *Figure 4.4*.

Saving a search

It is frequently possible to save a search stategy, either temporarily (e.g. for use later in the same week) or permanently (until erased). Permanent saving provides a current-awareness or SDI service, as the saved search formulation is executed every time there is a new update to the database. The saved search strategies can be purged at any time (*Figure 4.5*).

```
File411:DIALINDEX(tm)
(Copr. DIALOG Inf.Ser.Inc.)
? SELECTFILE BIOSCI
File5:BIOSIS PREVIEWS 81–85/Feb BA7903:RRM2803.
File34:SCISEARCH – 84/WK48
File55:BIOSIS Previews – 1977 thru 1980
File76:LIFE SCIENCES COLLECTION –78–84/Nov
File87:SCISEARCH – 81–83
File94:SCISEARCH – 78–80
File185:Zoological Record – 78–81/Dec
File186:SCISEARCH – 74–77
File238:TELEGEN – 73–84/Dec
File255:BIOSIS Previews – 1969 thru 1976
File310:CA Search – 1980–1981
File311:CA SEARCH 1982–84 UD=10202

    File Items Description
? S HERPESVIRUS
     (5)
                1213 HERPESVIRUS
     (34)
                 130 HERPESVIRUS
     (55)
                2985 HERPESVIRUS
     (76)
                3686 HERPESVIRUS
     (87)
                 415 HERPESVIRUS
     (94)
                 401 HERPESVIRUS
     (185)
                  46 HERPESVIRUS
     (186)
                 533 HERPESVIRUS
     (238)
                  12 HERPESVIRUS
     (255)
                4124 HERPESVIRUS
     (310)
                  93 HERPESVIRUS
     (311)
                 195 HERPESVIRUS
```

Figure 4.4 Searching the DIALOG biological database index

```
? END/SAVETEMP
Serial#T850
      25jan85 5:46:50 User7243
   $0.77 0.051 Hrs File154

? .RECALL T850
Line Set Command
   1   1   # HERPES GENITALIS
   2   2   # HERPES SIMPLEX
   3   3 C 1 AND 2
   4   4 C 1 OR 2
   5   5   # HERPESVIRUS INFECTIONS
   6   6 C 4 AND 5

? .RELEASE
Released T850
```

Figure 4.5 Using TEMPORARY SAVE to save a search strategy temporarily, by means of the RECALL statement and the RELEASE statement

Displaying a search strategy

If a very long and complicated search is carried out, it is easy to forget the stages in the search formulation. Some systems have a command which enables the searcher to display the previously selected sets of references (*Figure 4.6*).

```
? DISPLAY SETS
Set Items Description
  1    418 HERPES GENITALIS
  2   1656 HERPES SIMPLEX
  3     70 1 AND 2
  4   2004 1 OR 2
  5    727 HERPESVIRUS INFECTIONS
  6     55 4 AND 5
```

Figure 4.6 Using the DIALOG DISPLAY SETS statement to display a search strategy

Preparation of output

Some online systems enable users to organize the output according to various parameters. For example, in the DIALOG system, the command .SORT sorts the online output according to specified parameters; thus .SORT9/1–50/AU/TI sorts the first fifty items in set 9 into author order. In a similar way offline (i.e. printed) output can be sorted according to set parameters.

Document delivery

Many host systems enable users to order the source documents which have been found as a result of a search. This facility is very useful but expensive.

The process of first preparing an online search and then carrying it out is summarized in *Figure 4.7* (overleaf).

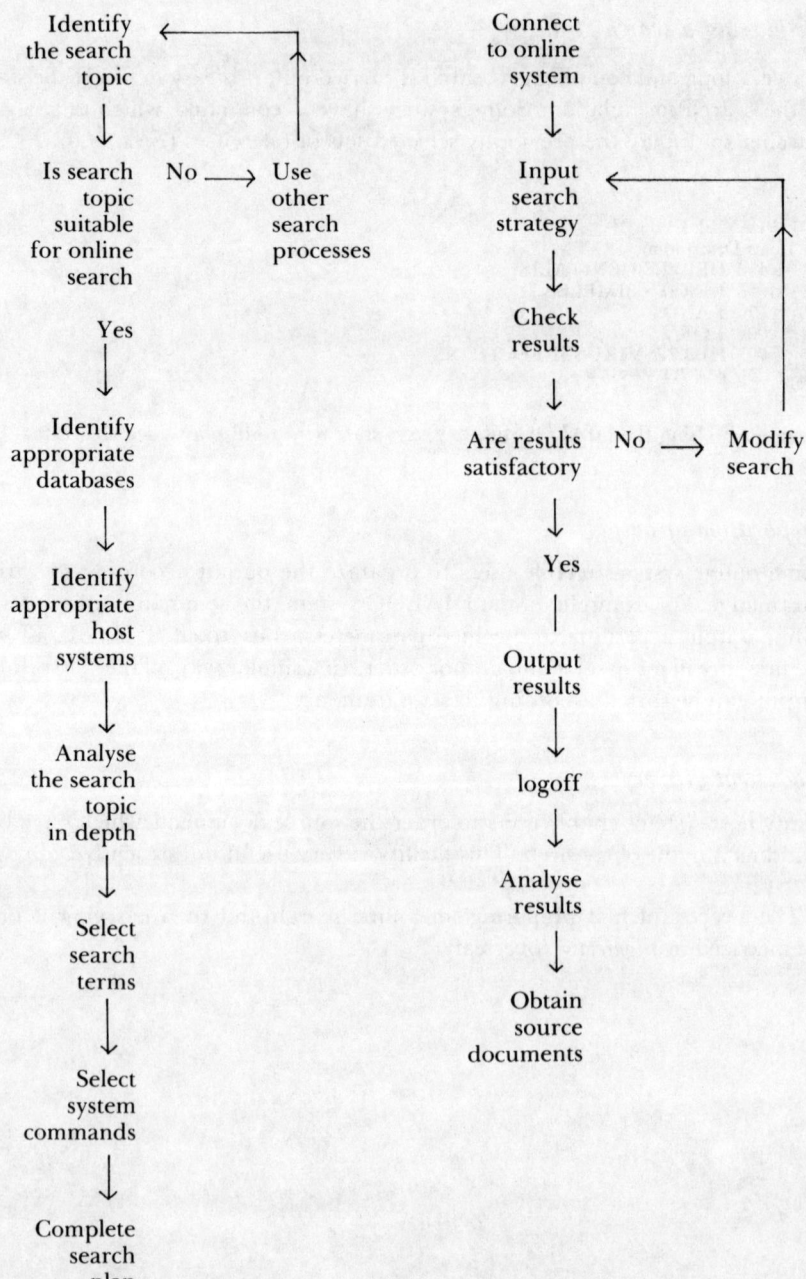

Figure 4.7 Summary of the techniques to be followed in online searching: preparing for a search; carrying out a search

5 Case studies

Throughout this book, we have mentioned sources of information useful to practitioners in medicine or medical information work. Search strategies have been outlined and techniques for online searching have been considered. The following sections include case studies where sources used by particular groups such as general practitioners and pharmacists are considered, as are the techniques for searching within a relatively narrow topic such as sickle cell anaemia. These latter searches are real in that they have been carried out for researchers in the field. None of the searchers had any subject knowledge. Finally, the problems of carrying out an online search in a multidisciplinary subject (toxicology) are considered in detail.

5.1 Sources used by general practitioners

In the course of his or her work, a general practitioner (GP) will require information in a number of medically related areas. Decisions regarding treatments, drug therapy and so on will be based on data of one kind or another. Much of this information will have been learned at medical school but new, potent medicines are becoming available all the time and sources will be needed. Of the various information sources outlined in the first two chapters of this book, only a small proportion will be readily available to GPs and so they will use other methods of staying up to date. Certain sources such as periodicals will always be a chosen source for obtaining evaluated drug information and sources such as *MIMS* will be used more than any other by the majority of GPs in their day-to-day prescribing.

General practitioners receive a large amount of unsolicited direct mail. It is advertising material sent with the aim of bringing the name of new products to the attention of GPs and to keep the name of established products in their mind. It arrives mainly from pharmaceutical companies and represents the investment of a large amount of money. The average general practitioner will receive every month in the region of thirty-six issues of controlled-circulation journals and thirty envelopes containing other direct mail.

The pharmaceutical representative

Each pharmaceutical company employs a sales force whose members are generally called representatives, reps or detail men, and additionally there are companies which hire out reps to drug companies when a new product is being promoted.

It is generally agreed that the representative has a greater effect than any other source when conveying information about *new* drugs. He is briefed on the products of a particular company but may only have a few minutes to get his message across. This means a careful organization of what needs the most promotion, and on that particular visit he may have to ignore other of the company's products.

The representative's assignment is to sell a product, yet many physicians accept the information as objective. However, one advantage of the rep over a hard-copy source is that questions can be asked and misunderstanding cleared. Not only does the rep bring information to the GP, he also reports back to the company about the response of the GP to the promoted product. In the United Kingdom the representative is expected to discuss his product in the light of currently available products. Of course he is bound to stress the advance represented by his product and is necessarily biased.

Colleagues

Apart from formal practice meetings which GPs attend, informal meetings within the practice and outside are important occasions for the interchange of ideas. Colleagues may be able to legitimize a GP's decision or may be able to change his prescribing of a new product.

External sources such as pharmacists

General practitioners tend to use easy-to-hand information and do not seek out external sources. The reasons for this pattern of usage are complex. However, some GPs no doubt find it psychologically difficult to contact, by telephone, an external source when a patient is sitting in the surgery, even though each pharmaceutical company has an information unit available to GPs, as do the larger hospitals in each region. Prestel may be able to overcome the problem by presenting the doctor with external information in a 'silent' manner. Moreover, patients may find the technological activity of the prescriber to be reassuring.

5.2 Searching for drug information

Many health care professionals will need to obtain information about drugs. The sources of information which they will use will include many of those previously mentioned. *Martindale* is a standard text in U.K. pharmacies, whether the high-street chemist or in the hospital. It is used for a number of reasons: to find old formulae, dosages or quite often to find the properties of a particular preparation. Its online equivalent will be used significantly in hospitals. Complex searches can be formulated and the service is updated regularly.

ABPI Data Sheet Compendium (London: Datapharm. Annual) is used to obtain information on specific preparations. Each data sheet included is prepared by the product's manufacturer and contains all the legally necessary information about that product. It can be useful in tracing a proprietary preparation when only the approved name is known.

The *British National Formulary* (*see* section 5.2) provides useful prescribing information. It gives the formulae of mixtures and includes a list of preparations available for dentists to prescribe within the National Health Service system. With its newly established twice-yearly frequency publication it has become a particularly useful source of information. Periodicals, abstracts and indexes, patents, etc. can all be used to obtain specific drug-related data.

There are one or two specific sources used in drug information units which have not been described in the more general first chapters. One of these is the IOWA Drug Information Service, also known by the initial letters IDIS. This service is provided from the University of Iowa and is a division of the College of Pharmacy. It was established in 1965 and one of its activities is the production of a Drug Literature Microfilm File. The yearly subscription covers the file, which consists of various indexes covering drugs and disease states and in particular, the full articles on microfilm. The provision of these full articles and indexes to the information held within them maintains the source's unique position in drug information.

Approximately 155 journals are selected and scanned for the IDIS service. They include a large number of English-language medical and pharmaceutical journals. All articles relating to drugs or drug therapy from these journals are included in full, and sections of the article are indexed for easy retrieval. As well as indexing drugs and disease states mentioned in the article, IDIS provides codes to identify details of therapy, pharmaceutics, toxicology, administration, incompatibilities and adverse effects, and the type of article.

Each article is identified by a code number, which is used to locate the microfilmed version of the article. These numbers are sequential, increasing at a rate of between 1,000 and 1,500 per month. The lag time between the publication of the original article and its indexing in the IDIS system is about three months, though some articles from the major weekly journals are included more rapidly. This rapid inclusion of full-text articles increases the service's usefulness to drug information specialists.

Both a Drug Name Index and a Diseases Index are available. The Drug Name Index uses generic drug names from the American Hospital Formulary Service (AHFS) and has a cross-reference index to help identify drug names which are not AHFS terminology. The Diseases Index uses nomenclature from the International Classification of Diseases, adapted. A complete list of all drug names and disease terms is included in the IDIS procedure manual, which should be consulted in the case of difficult search terms. The indexes for both drugs and diseases are cumulated annually and are updated monthly. The first edition of the index covers the years 1966 to 1973, thereafter each year has a separate cumulated index. Bibliographies on selected drugs are also prepared and issued with the monthly updates.

Sources used by pharmacists

Two sources of particular interest to retail pharmacists in the United Kingdom are the *British National Formulary* (*BNF*) and *OTC* (letters which generally stand for over-the-counter). The former is published jointly by the British Medical Association and the Pharmaceutical Society of Great Britain. It is now issued twice a year although at one time there was a gap of four or five years between editions, making it much less relevant than today.

The *BNF* includes guidance on prescribing classified notes on drugs and preparations. Drugs affecting particular body areas or systems are kept together, and an indication of the price range of each included drug is given. There is a formulary section which contains recipes for various preparations. At the back of the *BNF* is the Dental Practitioner's Formulary, which lists all preparations available for prescribing, by dentists, via the National Health Service. In addition to these particularly important sections, there are appendices covering intravenous additives, drug interactions and borderline substances, together with an index of manufacturers and a detailed subject index. The *BNF* has always been regarded highly by both GPs and pharmacists. The current twice-yearly publication schedule only goes to increase its usefulness.

OTC (London: Medical Publications), is a relatively new publication and is subtitled *The reference and prescribing aid for pharmacists*. It is laid out like *MIMS* and is edited by the same individual, and published monthly by the publishers of *MIMS* (Medical Publications Ltd.). It is available to pharmacists and other members of the medical professions. *OTC* lists all proprietary and generic medicines, dressings and appliances available in the United Kingdom which can be supplied without prescription from a registered pharmacy.

There are pages of news and comments which are followed by sections on the preparations themselves organized in terms of body areas, systems or diseases. Thus preparations for foot care are kept together, as are preparations for the relief of asthma and contact lens care preparations. There is a section for guidance on fees and endorsements for prescriptions and a very useful 'disallowed items' section covering items commonly disallowed by the Prescription Pricing Authority. By referring to this a great deal of irritation can be overcome. There is an index to *OTC* covering the manufacturers of the preparations and an alphabetical index of preparations, disorders, dressings, etc.

5.3 Case studies

The following searches, each in a narrow subject area, have been carried out for researchers in the field. The search strategy employed will be discussed. As none of the seachers had subject knowledge, basic sources such as dictionaries were needed to identify key terms and define difficult concepts. Each of the specialist researchers was sent, prior to the search, a brief questionnaire which asked for basic details, key references if available and the name of a good introductory textbook. In addition the researcher was asked what period and how many years should be searched and whether there were language restrictions or not.

Sickle cell anaemia: its management, control and prognosis
(James A. Parrish)

The first case study is for references on sickle cell anaemia, a search carried out for the Centre for Ethnic Minorities Health Studies in Bradford. (Full citations to the sources mentioned in this section are given in appropriate preceding chapters.)

A topic such as this covers a number of subject areas. Literature will be found in standard texts, reports and what is called the grey literature, which is poorly indexed, and poorly controlled in the bibliographic sense. The topic was first discussed with the Centre for Ethnic Minorities Health Studies to find the exact requirements of the researcher. A basic search strategy was compiled and worked through.

Dictionaries

Dictionaries were used to find suitable search terms, define new concepts and provide a basic lead in to the topic. Those chosen were as follows.

Butterworths medical dictionary. This proved difficult to use, as sickle cell anaemia was buried among the references on anaemia. Only a short definition was given.

Black's medical dictionary. This proved very useful and gave a good basic introduction via definitions. By following up the cross-references, the search could be widened to include all related topics.

Encyclopedias

The *McGraw-Hill encyclopedia of science and technology* provided a brief summary of the subject and suggested a few more search terms. However, when the information it provided was compared with that given in medical textbooks, it was seen not to be very useful. For the first definition of a new topic it was adequate.

Textbooks

Textbooks were traced by means of the *British National Bibliography (BNB)*. Using keywords within the subject index it was possible to find a number of textbooks on the subject. Those most useful were: Lehman, H. and Huntsman, R. G. *Man's haemoglobins* (North-Holland, 1974) and Weatherall, D. J. and Hardisty, R. M. (eds.), *Blood and its disorders* (Oxford: Blackwell, 1982).

Informal contacts

At this stage, armed with definitions and some basic ideas, we decided to discuss the topic with workers in the field, both medical specialists and information professionals. Further contacts were obtained from clinical haematologists, who also provided various references to articles. At this stage the *Medical register* was used to obtain the addresses of contacts given by the haematologists. No other directory was used in this particular search.

Abstracting and indexing services

By using *Ulrich's International periodicals directory*, useful abstracting services were found. For each of the periodical articles suggested by the various informal contacts, we looked up in *Ulrich* its journal of publication. At the end of each *Ulrich* entry was listed the indexing or abstract services which covered that particular journal. The following were traced by this method: *Index Medicus*, *Chemical Abstracts*, *Excerpta Medica*, *Biological Abstracts* and *Science Citation Index*. But since sickle cell anaemia as a topic is multifaceted, journals over the whole range of medicine, paramedicine and psychosocial medicine needed to be considered, and *Psychological Abstracts* was added to the list.

Bibliographies

To save time prior to an exhaustive search of the indexing and abstracting journals, we sought a published bibliography on the topic, but none was traced. Some broader topics were covered but many of the bibliographies concerned were out of date. It should be said that because of contacts made with workers in the field at the beginning of this search, a current bibliography was forwarded to the searcher from an earlier index.

Searching the indexes and abstracting services

Chemical Abstracts did not prove to be useful because it was, not surprisingly, chemically orientated, and the biochemical aspect of sickle cell anaemia was not of interest to this particular researcher.

As reviews are particularly useful it was decided to search for these first. The first method for finding reviews was to use the 'Bibliography of Medical Reviews' at the beginning of *Index Medicus*. All references located under the headings previously chosen were selected. A number of reviews were obtained, all under the two keywords ANEMIA and SICKLE CELL. Secondly, *Irregular serials and annuals* was used. Three useful titles were located under the general subject heading 'Medical Sciences' with the subheading 'Haematology'. All had been previously located using *Index Medicus* and *Biological Abstracts*.

Seven abstract journals or indexes were identified and checked for relevance: *Index Medicus*, *Excerpta Medica*, *Biological Abstracts*, *Psychological Abstracts*, *NLM Current Catalog*, *British Medicine* and *Science Citation Index*.

Index Medicus. Using MeSH the most specific term found was ANEMIA, SICKLE CELL, although a related term ANTISICKLING AGENTS was listed. Using the MeSH trees, relationships with other terms were discovered, but after discussion it was decided that the two terms just mentioned would be a sufficient basis for the search. A number of subheadings were considered useful as a means of refining it.

Excerpta Medica. The term SICKLE CELL ANEMIA was used to search. Two of the sections were found to be appropriate after using the *Guide to the classification and indexing system*—'Human Genetics' and 'Hematology'. *Excerpta Medica* was less extensive in its coverage of sickle cell anaemia and, as it is an abstracting rather than an indexing service, it appeared less up to date than *Index Medicus*. The extent of duplication between the two services was approximately forty percent.

Biological Abstracts. Using the *Guide to the vocabulary of 'Biological Abstracts'*, a list of search terms covering both the psychological and clinical aspects of the disease was constructed. SICKLE and ANEMIA were located in the KWIC index. Other search terms were also considered. Using the Concept Index each search term was used and abstract numbers were found, for the broad headings. From this the keyword index was used for a specific search.

We compared the abstract numbers from the concept index and the keyword index, and those which appeared in both were considered the most relevant. The search in *Biological Abstracts* was time-consuming and because of this source's emphasis on plant and animal biology, and general environmental aspects of biology, the number of relevant references retrieved was low. All those retrieved had previously been found using *Index Medicus*.

Psychological Abstracts. This was used to achieve a balance between the psychological and clinical aspects of the disease. The thesaurus of Psychological Index Terms was used to determine the search terms. The most specific term available was ANEMIA, but to cover the ethnic minorities aspect, the term ETHNIC GROUP was traced and the additional related terms were also noted. To encompass the control, management and prognosis of the disease, other terms were checked in the thesaurus. Eventually five key terms were selected for a search up to 1982 and an additional term SCREENING was used from 1982.

NLM Current Catalog. This source, although useful mainly for books, does index periodical articles to a lesser extent. After a careful search using a number of key terms, it was found that all relevant articles and monographs were located under the single term ANEMIA, SICKLE CELL. The *Catalog* is published only quarterly and therefore the articles are more out of date than those found in *Index Medicus*. Information retrieved from the *Current Catalog* did, however, yield a considerable amount of new material and showed little overlap with *Index Medicus*.

British Medicine. This was used to search for books. In this aspect of the search emphasis was placed on clinical medicine, biomedical sciences and the interdisciplinary subject areas.

Science Citation Index. For each reference provided by the researcher, *Science Citation Index* was used to trace any article which had cited it. These traced articles should be relevant to the search and as *Science Citation Index* is multidisciplinary, the coverage should be different from that provided by the sources already searched. Using the Permuterm Index, a subject approach was possible.

Bringing the search up to date

Current Contents. Using the subject index of the *Life Sciences* and *Clinical Practice* issues of *Current Contents*, a number of useful references were obtained. The author index was also useful; in searching the indexing and abstract services, a number of key authors had been noted and their names were looked up in *Current Contents*' author index.

Using the journals

By searching the literature, we became aware of the most frequently cited periodicals, the ones which produced the majority of the relevant references. These journals were scanned individually from the date of the last cited reference.

Other sources of information

Theses. In *Index of Theses*, the subject index was searched using the term SICKLE CELL. Very little information was retrieved and that which was had a clinical bias.

Dissertation Abstracts International. This is a difficult source to use over a period of time. In the monthly issues of category B, the nearest search term available was ANEMIA. However, once a reference was located, the words 'sickle cell' if present in the title showed its relevance.

British Reports, Translations and Theses. The keyword index was searched using the term SICKLE CELL ANAEMIA. Nothing was retrieved using this source that had not been retrieved by other means.

Research in Progress. We checked *Research in British universities, polytechnics and colleges* but using the term SICKLE CELL ANAEMIA gave no additional contacts.

Online searching

From the available databases, *Psychinfo* was rejected because of its poor coverage of the clinical and medical sciences and its high overlap with its printed version. *EMBASE*, too, was rejected but only for reasons of cost and because of its narrower coverage of the clinical sciences.

Medline was chosen because of its adequate, representative coverage of the subject, its moderate cost and the availability of MeSH headings and the other tools to aid searching. Some very useful additional references were retrieved by means of the online search.

Mental health and ethnic minorities in Britain (by Angela McHarron)

This was a search carried out for the Centre for Ethnic Minorities Health Studies in Bradford. As with the first case study, an initial questionnaire had provided some references to give the searcher a lead-in to the topic. After this, several guides were used to discover where relevant literature might be found.

Walford and Sheehy's *Guide to reference books* were useful to find titles of more specific guides although they did not indicate how useful these listed titles might be. Morton and Godbolt's *Information sources in the medical sciences* was found to be a good introduction to the literature, and it gave some indication as to how to use this literature. Elliott's *Guide to the documentation of psychology*, a 1971 publication, was very out of date and therefore was not used. *A brief guide to sources in science and technology*, by S. Herner, was no more useful than the original Morton and Godbolt.

The next stage was to identify terms for searching. There were three concepts in the original title: mental health, ethnic minorities and Britain. For the mental health aspect, *Black's medical dictionary* was used, as were MeSH headings, and a list of twenty-three terms was drawn up. For ethnic minorities using MeSH headings there were eleven possible terms. It was very difficult to identify terms exhaustively for the 'Britain' concept so general terms were used. The researcher at the Centre for Ethnic Minorities Health Studies was contacted at this stage, and a discussion led to the removal of the terms related to Britain.

Abstracting and indexing sources

The most useful abstracting and indexing sources were found using references originally supplied by the researcher. Key journals had been identified and *Ulrich* was used, as in the previous case study, to find the relevant abstracting and indexing journals. Seven possible sources were identified, the most frequently mentioned ones being *Index Medicus*, *Excerpta Medica* and *Psychological Abstracts*. An initial search through one year of each of these three was carried out and it showed that *Index Medicus* and *Excerpta Medica* were not producing as many references as had been expected. *Psychological Abstracts*, however, was shown to be very useful. *Biological Abstracts* was considered but searching it took up much too much time in relation to the number of articles it was producing. As *Index Medicus* and *Excerpta Medica* had not produced anything that *Psychological Abstracts* was not also producing, they were dropped from the search. A ten-year search through *Psychological Abstracts* was initiated although terms had now to be refined using the thesaurus. Most of the references eventually found came from this source.

The researcher was then contacted again to check on the relevance of the articles found, and irrelevant references were discussed. The search was continued using *Social Science Citation Index*. As many relevant articles had been found using the abstracting journals, an author approach was used to search this citation index. The ten most cited authors were used to trace articles; however, the search was long, laborious and not very productive and was abandoned after the examining of two years of the index.

Almost all of the material retrieved so far was in the form of journal articles or books, although there were only one or two of the latter. In order to widen the search, theses were traced. Using *Index to Theses* and *Dissertation Abstracts International*, ten theses were located via 'mental health' as the main concept. All of them had been written before 1981.

Conferences were located using *Index of Conference Proceedings Received by the BLL* (Boston Spa: British Library Lending Division) although these had already been traced using the other sources. Relevant meetings which had been held on the subject and had been found in references within some of the traced articles had not been indexed in this source.

Leeds University library staff keep a card index of conference proceedings in their collection and this was checked; nothing was found.

Current awareness

The most cited journals from the search were identified, and the most recent citation from each of these journals was also noted. The individual journals were then scanned for relevant articles, and about ten were found. *Current Contents* was used to check those journals which were not easily available or had been cited only once or twice during the search. The two parts of *Current Contents* used were *Clinical Practice* and *Life Sciences*. A year's issues were scanned, and this search produced three relevant articles from the *Life Sciences* part and two from *Clinical Practice*.

The above search retrieved about 350 articles altogether over the ten-year period investigated, and the searcher cut these down to about 125 references by editing out all articles more than three years old.

Problems encountered

The main problem was with the terminology. MeSH headings were used first and then it was discovered that *Psychological Abstracts* uses its own terms. The twenty-three terms from MeSH were cut to ten when using *Psychological Abstracts*. Within this source the terminology caused a problem as it kept changing over the years of the search. The group referred to in 1984 as BLACKS had been called NEGROES in 1981. As has been explained, the *Psychological Abstracts* thesaurus does give historical notes for guidance. RACIAL AND ETHNIC DIFFERENCES was a preferred term from 1982; prior to this the term was RACIAL DIFFERENCES.

In *Psychological Abstracts* it was easier and more effective to search using terminology for ethnic minorities than it was for specific mental health terms.

The researcher had restricted the search to articles in English, but it was irritating to the searcher that many apparently relevant articles were being ignored because they were in a foreign language. The index to *Psychological Abstracts* gives no indication as to the language of an article, and users need to turn to the abstract itself to discover this.

Psychological Abstracts is arranged in subject areas, and the topic was spread over a number of these. The contents pages showed the complete list of abstract numbers in each area. The searcher needed to check all abstracts identified in the index against the contents pages to ensure that they did in fact come from one of the relevant areas before looking them up, a somewhat time-wasting business.

The only other problems tended to be minor irritations such as the very small print in *Social Science Citation Index*.

The searches carried out for the Centre for Ethnic Minorities Health Studies formed part of a final-year degree assessment of the students concerned. For this reason a strict time limit was imposed and to some extent there was a source limitation also. The 'search technique' tutors did not wish to expand the search into the 'grey literature'; this aspect was to be covered by the Centre itself. Sources which might have been useful but which have not been discussed so far are:

Sage Race Relations Abstracts
Institute of Race Relations Library
Runnymede Trust Library

These are good for books and other literature where race is the main topic.

Central-government literature can be traced via the monthly and annual lists or the sectional lists of Her Majesty's Stationery Office (HMSO). There is also the *Catalogue of British official publications not published by HMSO* (Cambridge: Chadwyck-Healey, 1984). Local-government information related to race and race relations can be found using the Local Authorities Race Relations Information Exchange (LARRIE) and social or voluntary work can be traced in *Social Services Abstracts, Social Work Information Bulletin* and *Voluntary Forum Abstracts*.

For the work to be maintained, communication is essential. Contact with individuals, groups and organizations active in the sphere of health and ethnic minorities is very important, and is made easier by subscribing to newsletters, bulletins, etc. Also, it is important to attend relevant meetings, conferences, seminars and workshops so that new contacts can be made and old contacts reaffirmed. Good contacts with local authorities, Health Education Units and Community Relations Councils should be maintained, as should contacts with black community groups and community health projects.

Glucocorticoid receptors (by Sharon Lerch)

The third search was carried out for the Department of Animal Physiology and Nutrition at Leeds University. The initial questionnaire responses made it clear that the researcher was looking at the action of glucocorticoid receptors with the aim of finding an antagonist to cortisol using rat muscle. The searcher was asked to include all rodents, cattle, birds (particularly the chicken) and the human. The years to be studied would be from 1975 to the present and only references in English were to be retrieved. After a very brief search of the literature, the researcher was again contacted and the irrelevant references discarded. This helped refine the search terms in the searcher's mind.

Dictionaries, textbooks and encyclopedias

Butterworths medical dictionary was very useful in providing a basic definition, in simple terms, of receptors, steroids, glucocorticoids and cortisol. It was used at the beginning of the search and whenever a term in a periodical article title was unknown.

Textbooks. Those used were general textbooks on anatomy and physiology; more than one was used to provide a slightly different emphasis. They provided a sound background to the subject and enabled search terms to be identified. A textbook on cellular receptors was used to provide basic information on receptors from which more search terms were identified.

Abstracts and indexes

Before searching abstracting and indexing journals, MeSH headings were used in order to find the correct headings for searching *Index Medicus* and additional terms with which to search. Using the references provided initially by the researcher, and by using *Ulrich*, five services were located. These were *Index Medicus, Excerpta Medica, Current Contents, Biological Abstracts* and *Chemical Abstracts*.

Index Medicus. The search was taken from the 1984 monthly issues to the cumulative yearly issues back to 1975 using seven chosen keywords. Terms changed over the period, and care was needed to identify the changes using MeSH. Overall the most relevant search terms were GLUCOCORTICOID RECEPTORS, STEROID and RECEPTORS, HORMONE (pre-1977).

The review articles were checked first, then the individual citations. Initially 200 references were retrieved but, after discussions with the researcher, over half were rejected as they were irrelevant.

Excerpta Medica. Using the *Guide to the classification and indexing system* sections relevant to the search were located. 'Physiology' was the most relevant section for MUSCLE AND TENDON RECEPTORS, whereas GLUCOCORTICOIDS was located in the 'Pharmacology' section. Terms located in MeSH were not relevant for the *Excerpta Medica* search, for which broader headings were used. No new references were located.

Biological Abstracts. Using the keyword subject index, key terms were located. Two years were searched and, as no new references were located, no further years were searched.

Bringing the search up to date

Current Contents. The *Clinical Practice* section was not relevant to this search so only *Life Sciences* was searched. Specific terms were located in the keyword index. The search was time-consuming as each weekly issue had to be scanned, although the cumulative issues helped. Again, the most recent relevant article traced using the abstract journals was used as a starting point or, more correctly, an ending point for the *Current Contents* search. *Current Contents* was useful for a quick, up-to-date search.

Current journals. The journals containing the most relevant references were checked from the date of the most recent article retrieved to the present date. By chance, an advertisement was noticed for a new book on glucocorticoid antagonists. One or two relevant articles were also found.

Theses

Index to Theses. Four years of this index were searched using various terms. Three relevant theses were located and included in the bibliography.

Dissertation Abstracts International. No relevant theses were located.

British Reports, Translations and Theses. Three years were checked; twenty-nine possible references were located and on investigation one of these proved relevant.

Conference proceedings

British Library Index to Conference Proceedings. A large number of apparently relevant references were located which had to be obtained from the British Library Lending Division. None of the proceedings proved to be relevant to the researcher.

Research in progress

Using *Research in British universities, polytechnics and colleges* two relevant research centres were found. These are of course useful as a means of finding contact persons and it might have been better to have looked at this source prior to any other.

Effect of infection on wound healing (by Brigitte Lawson)

The topic given by the researcher for this literature search was 'the effect of infection on wound healing'. The researcher identified the following key terms: wound infection, wound healing, leg ulcer, decubitus ulcer, skin ulcer, microbiology, bacteriology, skin lesion, burns and surgical wounds. The researcher also stated that she wanted the literature search to go back to 1960 and to be restricted to English-language articles.

The searcher used *Black's medical dictionary* to clarify the meaning of the terms she received from the researcher, and also to identify any other suitable terms or synonyms which might be needed in the search. This dictionary provided simple and clear descriptions of the keywords and enabled the searcher to obtain a clear picture of the subject.

The next step was to identify a guide to the medical literature and sources, and the catalogue of the medical library indicated the existence of Morton and Goldbolt's *Information sources in the medical sciences.* The searcher found this book valuable as it provided a broad base on which to start searching and allowed her to identify a range of useful sources. The sources which were identified as being useful for the retrospective search were *Index Medicus, Excerpta Medica, Biological Abstracts, Nursing Research Abstracts, International Nursing Index, Science Citation Index, Index to Conference Proceedings, Index to Theses* and *Dissertation Abstracts.* The use of each of these sources will be described individually.

Index Medicus

In order to search *Index Medicus* it is necessary to find the appropriate subject headings. Using MeSH the following headings were thought relevant to this particular search: WOUND HEALING; WOUND INFECTION; SURGICAL WOUND INFECTION; DECUBITUS ULCER; BACTERIAL INFECTION; SKIN ULCER; and BURNS. The cross-references in MeSH were checked but none of the entries was found to be relevant to this search. The Tree Structures were also looked at to see whether they could be used to make the search more specific, but they revealed that the search terms chosen were already sufficiently specific.

Each of the seven relevant headings had to be searched in the annual cumulated indexes going back to 1960. Within each of the main headings were subsections: for example,

Wound healing
   Prevention and control
   Physiology
   Effect of drugs (etc.)

The use of the subsection enabled the searcher to omit irrelevant groups of entries. To bring the *Index Medicus* search up to date, the searcher used the monthly volumes.

Excerpta Medica

Using the *Guide to the classification and indexing system* and the Index, the searcher looked up the terms WOUND HEALING, WOUND INFECTION and SURGICAL WOUND INFECTION, and found the following entries:

WOUND HEALING   1, 5, 9, 34, 37
WOUND INFECTION   4, 9
SURGICAL WOUND INFECTION *use* WOUND INFECTION

The number refer to the printed sections of *Excerpta Medica* and the searcher identified the following sections as being most useful:

  4   Microbiology
  9   Surgery
34   Plastic surgery

While the other sections might have been usefully searched, the searcher did not have sufficient time.

The retrospective search involved using the index at the back of each annual cumulation to see what items on wound healing and wound infection were included. As keywords are given, the searcher could see at a glance if there were any relevant items. If there were, they were checked by reading the abstract. The monthly sections were then searched.

As compared with *Index Medicus*, it was found that *Excerpta Medica* had the following advantages:

1. Keywords enable one to identify what an article is about.
2. Abstracts are given in many cases.
3. The search can be more specialized because of the division of the abstracts into sections.

However, the following points were also noted when searching *Excerpta Medica* as compared with *Index Medicus*:

1. It was more time-consuming to have to search three sections per year.
2. The search did not provide as many references.

Nursing Research Abstracts

Nursing Research Abstracts required a different search technique and it was necessary to search through the uncontrolled subject index for each year. The keywords used in the search were those provided by the researcher and MeSH, but the search provided few references and was stopped after the years 1983–1979 had been searched.

International Nursing Index

The *International Nursing Index* was easy to use as its organization was based on that of MeSH. The same MeSH headings were used in the search—which proved to be quick and fairly productive—as had been used for *Index Medicus*.

Biological Abstracts

The searcher found *Biological Abstracts* to be a very useful source but had time to search only the most recent two years. Using the subject index, she looked up the search terms and as it is a keyword-in-context (KWIC) index she was able to scan the other elements given and decide whether or not a particular entry was likely to be relevant. If it did appear to be relevant then its abstract could be found using the entry number.

Science Citation Index

SCI was used to trace articles which cite the work of a few key authors (such as T. K. Hunt and R. F. Edlich) who were identified by the searcher. It proved to be a useful source: the 1983 volume indicated that forty-one authors had cited T. K. Hunt. This enabled a useful pattern of references to be extracted.

Index to Conference Proceedings Received by the BLL; Index to Theses; Dissertation Abstracts

These three sources were searched using the subject terms WOUND HEALING and WOUND INFECTION and provided a number of useful references which had not been picked up from other sources.

Updating the search

The search was updated to bring in current references using *Current Contents* and primary journals. Two sections of *Current Contents*, namely *Clinical Practice* and *Life Sciences*, were checked by searching for the keywords in the subject index and then looking at the relevant page for the entry. This search was then updated to cover those items that had not been covered by the most recent issues of *Current Contents* and five key journals fall into this category: *Surgical Forum, Surgery, Gynecology and Obstetrics, New England Journal of Medicine, American Journal of Surgery* and *Journal of Dermatologic Surgery and Oncology*.

5.4 Searching a multidisciplinary subject: toxicology

This section describes the searching of online databases for toxicological information and is based largely on a British Library report (King, 1983).

Toxicology is a multidisciplinary subject with a large and widely scattered literature, consequently many online databases contain toxicological information and when searching in this field it is often difficult to decide which of them is the most appropriate. The aims of the British Library study were to compare the major databases in the field, to investigate their relative strengths and weaknesses, and to suggest situations where one might be preferred to others. This study is of interest to the online searcher as it indicates many practical problems and solutions to online searching which are relevant not only to the field of toxicology but that of medicine.

The online search used in this study were *Toxline, Medline, Cancerlit, EMBASE, CA Search, BIOSIS Previews* and *International Pharmaceutical Abstracts*. The databases selected were examined and analysed for their subject coverage in the field of toxicology and also their search facilities specific to toxicology. King summarized the report's findings in *Tables 5.1* and *5.2*. The performance of each of these databases was then evaluated in terms of recall, precision, overlap, currency and failure. Recall can be expressed quantitatively as:

$$\text{Recall} = \frac{\text{No. of relevant documents retrieved}}{\text{Total no. of relevant documents}} \times 100$$

This recall ratio expresses the ability of the system to retrieve documents relevant to an enquiry. In this study 'relative recall', by which is meant the measurement of the ability of a system to retrieve relevant documents as compared with the other systems involved in the investigation, is used to compare this aspect of database performance.

$$\text{Relative recall} = \frac{\text{No. of relevant documents retrieved by one system}}{\text{Total no. of relevant documents retrieved by all systems}} \times 100$$

The precision ratio can be expressed as:

$$\text{Precision} = \frac{\text{No. of relevant documents retrieved}}{\text{Total no. of documents retrieved}} \times 100$$

Table 5.1. Summary of searching features specific to toxicology

From King (1983), courtesy of the British Library

Data file	Forms of indexing thesaurus	Searching features specific to toxicology
Toxline	Uncontrolled vocabulary. TW from titles, keywords and abstract. CAS registry number, trade name, synonyms from *Chemline* file. Data tags and index tags.	Subfile searching. Pesticide toxicity—HAYES, PESTAB and HAPAB. Mutagenicity—EMIC. Teratogenicity—ETIC, TERA. Data tags (CTD Chronic toxic dose; LC; LD; TD Teratogenic dose). Index tags CARC carcinogens. MUTA.
Medline	Controlled and free-text searching on title and abstract from 1975. MeSH headings, subheadings, MeSH class number, check tags.	MeSH heading TOXICOLOGY, TOXIC, CARCINOGENS, MUTAGENS, TERATOGENS, etc. Subheadings (i) ADVERSE EFFECTS, POISONING and TOXICOLOGY applied to main heading; (iii) DRUG EFFECTS applied to main heading for organ.
CA Search	CACon uncontrolled. CASIA controlled. Keyword index terms from title, text or content of document. CAS registry numbers, index names, synonyms, MF, CA section numbers.	*CA* index terms—toxicity, toxicology, poisons, poisoning, carcinogen mutagens, teratogenesis, safety, health hazard. *CA* sections CA004 Toxicology; CA059 Air pollution and industrial hygiene.
BIOSIS	Controlled vocabulary, Keywords, descriptors Concept codes, concept names. Taxonomic codes.	Cross codes CC00531 Forensic science; Toxicology section CC22501–22506, CC24007 Carcinogens and carcinogenesis; CC25552 Descriptive teratology, CC25554 Experimental teratology; CC35500 Allergy and CC37013 Occupational health. Biosystematic code BC86215 Hominidae.
IPA	Controlled vocabulary. Descriptors. Pharmacological classification (AHFS system). Section heading.	*IPA* sections. Adverse drug reaction; Drug interactions; Drug metabolism and body distribution; Environmental toxicity; Toxicity.
Excerpta Medica	Controlled vocabulary. Preferred terms (MALIMET) plus secondary terms (uncontrolled). Section classification. EMTAGS—'item index'.	*EM* sections: 30 Pharmacology and toxicology; 38 Adverse reactions titles; 37 Drug literature index; 16 Cancer; 17 Public health, social medicine and hygiene; 35 Occupational health and industrial medicine; 46 Environmental health and pollution control; 49 Forensic science abstracts; 40 Drug dependence; 21 Developmental biology and teratology; 22 Human genetics. Item index: 302 Intoxication and poisoning; 315 Congenital defects; 198 Drug adverse reactions; 210 Forensic medicine; 300 Iatrogenic disease; 800 Normal humans.

Table 5.1.—Continued

Data file	Forms of indexing thesaurus	Searching features specific to toxicology
Cancerline	CANCERLIT uncontrolled and free-text searching. CANCERPROJ controlled and free-text searching of title, summary or index terms. Subject captions. Hierarchical subject codes.	All cancer-related material.
CIS Abstracts (manual)	CIS Thesaurus (1974) approx. 5,000 terms. Main and secondary descriptors.* 39 specific categories. Subject index—main descriptors, indexing titles and CIS accession no. (no. of descriptors/document =10–15).	
IDIS (manual)	Generic drug name indices (AHFS TERMS). Clinical disease term indices (ICD.9.CM terms).	ICD.9.CM terms. Toxicity, unclass chemicals; disease state—drug induced; allergic disorders, drugs. Descriptors: side effect/adverse reaction, toxicology.

*CAS registry numbers are used as secondary descriptors whenever a chemical substance is indexable. The secondary descriptors are only machine-readable.

This ratio expresses the efficiency with which the system achieves a particular recall ratio.

Overlap can easily be evaluated by comparing the number of relevant references retrieved by one database that are also retrieved by another in the same subject category.

Currency, as measured by the amount of time that elapses between the publication of a document and its appearance in a secondary source, is an important aspect of any information retrieval system, particularly in a fast-moving subject such as toxicology, where information searchers may require up-to-date information for immediate clinical application. Currency can be measured by comparing the publication date of references to their date of first appearance in the database. This measure of currency may be misleading as true currency is the date of appearance in the database as compared to the date the reference was *received* by the database producer.

Failure analysis involves identifying all the relevant documents which were *not* retrieved and if possible establishing why they were not retrieved. The indexing language seems to be the most important factor, as both indexers and searchers can perform only as well as the indexing language will permit.

Table 5.2. Subject contribution of the databases to toxicology
From King (1983), courtesy of the British Library

Data file	Relative contribution to different areas of toxicology
Toxline	All types of toxicology search. Subfiles specific to different areas include: Pesticide toxicity — HAYES, HAPAB, PESTAB Experimental toxicology — EMIC, ETIC, TERA Chemical hazards — CBAC, HEEP Drug-related toxicology — IPA, TOXBIB
BIOSIS	Experimental toxicology, some chemical and clinical toxicology. Covers all biological aspects. Useful for techniques and methods for measurement of pollutants.
CA Search	Experimental toxicology and chemical hazards. Specific substance indexing including registry numbers, therefore useful in all chemically related areas. Subsections on agrochemical toxicity, carcinogens and industrial hygiene.
Cancerlit	All cancer-related material
CIS Abstracts	All aspects of occupational medicine and industrial toxicology.
Excerpta Medica	Clinical and experimental toxicology; adverse reactions of drugs. Occupational, environmental and forensic aspects. Cancer-related material, mutagenesis, teratogenesis.
IDIS	Drug-related toxicology, side effects, adverse reactions, interactions in humans; limited amount of non-drug toxicology; drug treatment of toxicity poisoning.
IPA	Drug-related material including adverse drug reactions, drug interactions and drug metabolism.
Medline	Clinical and experimental toxicology including a large amount of cancer-related material. Also useful for specific toxic effects or a particular type of hazard, e.g. occupational dermatitis; use of 'chemically induced' for diseases, syndromes, congenital abnormalities or symptoms caused by chemical compounds.

The study by King involved detailed investigation and comparison of a large number of retrospective searches and a number of current-awareness profiles on the selected databases. The detailed research results are too extensive to describe here and the reader is referred to the research reports. However, we shall examine a selection of the report's findings along with its main conclusion.

The results shown in *Table 5.3* were obtained for searching for information on 'short-term screening of carcinogens'. They indicate the large differences between the different databases. Note that while *Cancerlit* has the highest recall ratio, 277 of the articles were irrelevant.

As a result of their detailed investigation into the recall and precision of the different databases, the researchers concluded:

All the databases studied here can provide some information on most types of

Table 5.3. Recall and precision ratios for 'Short-term screening of carcinogens'

	Cancerlit	Medline	Toxline	Excerpta Medica
Total number of references retrieved	369	40	157	68
A*	44	15	57	13
B*	48	9	28	19
C*	277	16	72	36
Percentage precision (A)	11.9	50.0	26.3	19.1
Percentage precision (A and B)	24.9	80.0	54.1	47.0
Percentage recall (A)	41.9	14.2	54.2	12.3
Percentage recall (A and B)	46.7	12.1	43.1	16.2

* (A) refers to directly relevant references, (B) to partially relevant ones, and (C) to irrelevant references as graded by participants in the research.

toxicological query. The degree of recall and precision will vary with the database and the subject area.

The recall figures obtained throughout searching are never sufficiently high to recommend that searching one database is sufficient to provide a comprehensive cover of the literature for any query. A complementary combination of databases will always provide better results, in spite of the overlap that may occur. Even such a combination of databases may not give complete recall for topics which are well documented.

Most toxicology queries, unlike other subject areas, require comprehensive recall, and in some cases database searches should be supplemented by referral to standards, handbooks and other reference material.

Sometimes, databases are not the most appropriate source available. For example, topics of an analytical nature may be better suited to search on a data bank, or other compilation of evaluated information, e.g. Registry of Toxic Effects of Chemical Substances (RTECS).

Other topics not suitable for database searching include queries requiring older material or extremely recent articles. In the latter case, the searcher could obtain more profitable results by referring to *Current Contents* or directly searching the core journals of the subject area.

Their conclusions with respect to overlap of the databases were that:

The overlap varies between the same files in different subject areas. *Toxline* generally has a high overlap with the main files from which its component files are derived. The overlap reaches 100% between *Toxline* and *IPA*. The incomplete overlap between *Toxline* and the files which contribute to it indicates that both *Toxline* and the 'parent' files, i.e. *Medline*, *BIOSIS* and *CA Search*, can be searched in combination and that each is able to provide unique relevant references. A different recall is obtained from *Toxline* for two reasons. The first relates to the difference in indexing between the 'parent' file and the *Toxline* sub-file, e.g. *HEEP* and *BIOSIS*, where CAS registry numbers are and are not present, respectively. The second reason is that the transfer of toxicology-related articles from the 'parent' file to *Toxline* is incomplete. Some articles may not be transferred if they were originally entered into the parent file in a section or with keywords that are not automatically considered as *Toxline* material.

These conclusions are illustrated by the results of one of the overlap studies, namely that on drug-related toxicology, as shown in *Table 5.4*.

The investigation indicated that the currency of the databases varies and it was suggested that '*Medline* contains the most current literature while *Excerpta Medica* is significantly less current than all the other databases'.

The results of the failure analysis are summarized in *Table 5.5*.

Table 5.4. Results of overlap study. Category 1: Drug-related toxicology
From King (1983), courtesy of the British Library

Database sampled	Number of references in sample	Number of references covered by each database and percentage overlap									
		Toxline		Medline		Excerpta Medica		BIOSIS		IPA	
		No.	%	No.	%	No.	%	No.	%	No.	%
Toxline	75	–	–	58	77.3	48	64.0	45	60.0	17	22.6
Medline	75	63	84.0	–	–	50	66.5	44	58.6	19	25.3
Excerpta Medica	75	48	64.0	42	56.0	–	–	26	34.6	12	16.0
BIOSIS	75	46	61.3	54	72.0	43	57.3	–	–	7	9.3
IPA	38	38	100.0	30	78.9	29	76.3	24	63.1	–	–

Table 5.5. Analysis of search failures
From King (1983), courtesy of the British Library

Reason for failure	CA Search	Toxline	BIOSIS	Medline	Excerpta Medica	Cancerlit	IPA
Strategy too general	2	–	1	–	–	–	2
Strategy too specific	2	9	6	6	4	9	3
Strategy completely at variance with the indexing	–	–	–	–	6	–	3
Indexing at fault	1	–	–	2	–	–	–
Currency	4	–	3	2	–	1	2
Inexplicable	1	1	–	–	–	–	–
Total number of references	10	10	10	10	10	10	10

The research workers concluded that:

> The main reason for failure on all databases is the inability to construct search strategies that will retrieve references at all levels of specificity, which is in turn due to inflexibility or lack of structure in the indexing language.
>
> A thorough understanding of the index language and database construction can greatly assist the formulation of good search strategies. Knowledge of the hard copy equivalent and constant referral to it can also help in the construction of profiles, since the searcher is likely to know the sort of information that each section heading will retrieve. This point also emphasizes the need to make thorough use of user aids.

King provides a useful set of general guidelines for toxicology searching which include the following points:

A toxicology topic frequently consists of two distinct components: a chemical substance and a toxic effect. When searching for a chemical substance it is best to search a database which uses CAS registry numbers (the *Chemical Abstracts* substrate reference numbers), such as *CA Search* or *Toxline*. These databases should be searched using CAS registry numbers and chemical names and synonyms taking into account how individual systems treat compound chemical names. For generic substance searching, a group of terms must be entered on all the databases searched and this group should at least include the names of the major specific substances. *Medline* is very useful when searching for generic substances as some compound classes, especially drugs, are represented as MeSH headings. The 'explode' facility can be used to include all the specific substances simply and automatically. If the search topic includes a particular preparation then it is necessary to search for the toxicity of this substance using both the preparation's name and also those of its major components.

When searching for a specific toxic effect, the most suitable databases will be those where specific effects can be expressed accurately, namely *Medline* or *Excerpta Medica*. (It is worth noting that since this research was published *BIOSIS* has also had these facilities added.) King states:

> It can be more difficult to search for general toxic effects or 'all toxicology' of a given substance than for specific effects.

This type of search requires a detailed profile of search terms to be entered in all databases.

To summarize, searching for information in a multidisciplinary subject involves following the guidelines given in the section on online searching strategy, and also using the detailed experience of other workers. In the field of toxicology the work of King has given much useful information and her bibliography also provides access to further literature on this subject. It is worth while to remember that the detail of the structure and methods of accessing different databases are continually changing, and it is often advisable to contact the database provider to obtain up-to-date advice on the best searching techniques.

Reference

King, Jane. *Searching international databases: a comparative evaluation of their performance in toxicity*. Boston Spa: British Library, 1983. Library and Information Research Report 3.

6 Organizing medical information

The previous chapters describe in some detail the processes involved in finding medical information. It must be obvious to anyone reading these chapters that a search for information can be an expensive and time-consuming business. Once we have obtained the desired information it is likely that we will want to store it so that it can be referred to when required. This chapter is concerned with organizing our information, whether in the form of bibliographic references or raw data, in an efficient manner.

Information can be stored in either a manual or a computerized system. A simple manual system may be created by organizing information on a set of 5 × 3 in ($12\frac{1}{2}$ × $7\frac{1}{2}$ cm) cards stored in a record drawer. Simple record systems can also be created using a microcomputer with an appropriate software package, as will be described later in this chapter. We will start by looking at some of the fundamental characteristics of systems for organizing information.

6.1 Information records

The basis of any information retrieval system, whether manual or computerized, is the record. Computer scientists may argue this point with respect to relational databases but it holds true for all manual systems and the vast majority of computerized systems.

A typical record can be defined in the following way:

Record. The total structure.
Field. A subsection of a record.
Field name. The name assigned to a field.
Field size. The amount of space which has been assigned to a field. In a manual system, this may be one or several spaces or lines on a card. In a computerized system, the field size may be fixed or variable. If the latter, the end of the field must normally be marked with an end-of-field indicator.
Data. The contents of the field. Data may be numeric (i.e. have a numeric value and therefore capable of being used in calculations) or data may be alphanumeric.

In the example shown in *Figure 6.1*, the record for a computerized system has a fixed field structure. The size of each field is given in numbers and is equivalent to the number of alphanumeric or punctuation characters that can be input into each field. The size of each record can be calculated by adding together the field sizes. In this example, the record size is 15 + 30 + 2 + 10 + 4 + 30 = 91 characters. In computer terms this is equivalent to 91 bytes.

```
┌─────────────────────────────────────────────────┐
│                                                 │
│    AUTHOR                                       │
│    TITLE                                        │
│                                                 │
│    EDITION                                      │
│                                                 │
│    PUBLISHER                        DATE        │
│                                                 │
│    NOTES                                        │
│                                                 │
│                                                 │
└─────────────────────────────────────────────────┘
```

Figure 6.1a Example records for a manual information retrieval system

```
AUTHOR. . . . . . . . . . . . . . . . . . . . . . . . . . . . . . . . . . . . . . . . . . . . (15)
TITLE . . . . . . . . . . . . . . . . . . . . . . . . . . . . . . . . . . . . . . . . . . . . . . . .
. . . . . . . . . . . . . . . . . . . . . . . . . . . . . . . . . . . . . . . . . . . . . . . . (30)
EDITION. . . . . . . . . . . . . . . . . . . . . . . . . . . . . . . . . . . . . . . . . . . . (2)
PUBLISHER . . . . . . . . . . . . . . . . . . . . . . . . . . . . . . . . . . . . . . . . . (10)
DATE . . . . . . . . . . . . . . . . . . . . . . . . . . . . . . . . . . . . . . . . . . . . . . (4)
NOTES . . . . . . . . . . . . . . . . . . . . . . . . . . . . . . . . . . . . . . . . . . . . . . .
. . . . . . . . . . . . . . . . . . . . . . . . . . . . . . . . . . . . . . . . . . . . . . . . (30)
```

Figure 6.1b Example records for a computerized information retrieval system

6.2 Contents of information records

The contents of information records will vary depending on the purpose of the file. It is worth spending some time, before establishing the file, in working out the parameters of the record. It is particularly important to do so in the case of computerized systems, where it may be difficult or even impossible to change the record structure once it has been established. *Tables 6.1–6.5* show how the purpose of an information retrieval system dictates the content of the records.

Table 6.1. A record suitable for storing journal references for a personal file

Field Name	Content
AUTHOR	Author's names, i.e. surnames and either initials or forenames.
TITLE	Title of the article as written by the author.
CITATION	Journal title, volume, issue, year and pagination.
SUBJECT NOTES	Brief notes outlining subject(s) covered by the article.
SOURCE	Citation of abstracting or indexing journal which included the article. Abstract number.

Table 6.2. Example record of the type shown in Table 6.1

GRANOFF, A.

Herpes virus and the Lucke tumor.
Cancer Research, 33(6) 1983, 1431–1433.
Rana pipiens (frog) is host to a renal adenocarcinoma (Lucke tumor).
Investigates relationship between temperature and the presence or absence
of herpes virus in tumor cells.
Excerpta Medica. Cancer 26(7), 1974, p. 449. (2612).

Table 6.3. A record suitable for storing journal references for an information service

Field Name	Content
ACCESSION NUMBER	Unique identification number of the record.
AUTHOR	Name of author(s) or corporate body responsible for the item.
TITLE	Title of the article as written by the author (or its translation).
SOURCE INFORMATION	For a book: edition, place of publication, publisher.
	For a journal: title, volume issue, pagination.
DATE	Year of publication.
DESCRIPTORS	Subject of the item. This may be expressed using a classification code, a term from a thesaurus, or a natural-language term.
LANGUAGE	Language of item.
SOURCE	Citation of abstracting or indexing journal which included the article. Abstract number.
ABSTRACT	A detailed summary of the content of the item.

Table 6.4. Example record of the type shown in Table 6.3

No. 152
ASANO, T.   OGASAWARA, N.

Stimulation of GABA receptor binding by barbiturates. *European Journal of Pharmacology*, 77(4), 355–357.
1982
DESCRIPTORS: Barbiturates; GABA receptor binding; bovine cerebral cortex membranes
English
Excerpta Medica. Pharmacology, 57(1), 1983, p. 21 (88).
Barbiturates increase Na^+-independent GABA binding to bovine cerebral cortex membranes. The relative activity of a series of compounds to enhance GABA binding correlates significantly with their anesthetic activity and with their ability to reverse bicuculline antagonism of GABA responses. There are regional differences in the maximal per cent stimulation of GABA binding by pentobarbital; a low stimulation in cerebellum.
(*Excerpta Medica* abstract)

Table 6.5. A record suitable for storing pharmaceutical information

Field Name	Content
BRAND NAME	The manufacturer's name for the product.
MANUFACTURER	The name of the manufacturer.
ACTIVE INGREDIENTS	The pharmacologically active ingredients of the product.
PRESENTATION	Physical presentation of the product.
INDICATIONS	Uses of the product.
PACKS AND PRICES	Mode of packaging and prices.
ADULT'S DOSE	Normal adult dosage.
CHILD'S DOSE	Normal children's dosage.
CONTRA-INDICATIONS	Circumstances when it should not be used.
SPECIAL PRECAUTIONS	Any special precautions which should be noted with the product.

Table 6.6. Example record of the type shown in Table 6.5

BRAND NAME	Sylopal.
MANUFACTURER	Norton
ACTIVE INGREDIENTS	Dimethicone 125 mg, Light mag. oxide 70 mg, alum. hydrox. gel to 5 ml
PRESENTATION	Suspension.
INDICATIONS	Flatulence, hyperacidity, heartburn.
PACKS AND PRICES	300 ml, £1.25
ADULT'S DOSE	5–10 ml before meals and at bedtime
CHILD'S DOSE	Not recommended
CONTRA-INDICATIONS	None
SPECIAL PRECAUTIONS	None

6.3 Subject access to information

The majority of researchers require subject access to their record systems. There are a number of possible approaches to subject access and each has its own advantages and disadvantages. It is beyond the scope of this book to describe the main systems but clear descriptions with special reference to personal documentation systems can be found in a book by Stibic (1980).

Serial files

The simplest method of organizing records is in a serial file, in which one record is stored after another one (*Figure 6.2*). This method is used in traditional library catalogues and is suitable for use in personal manual information retrieval

Organizing medical information 131

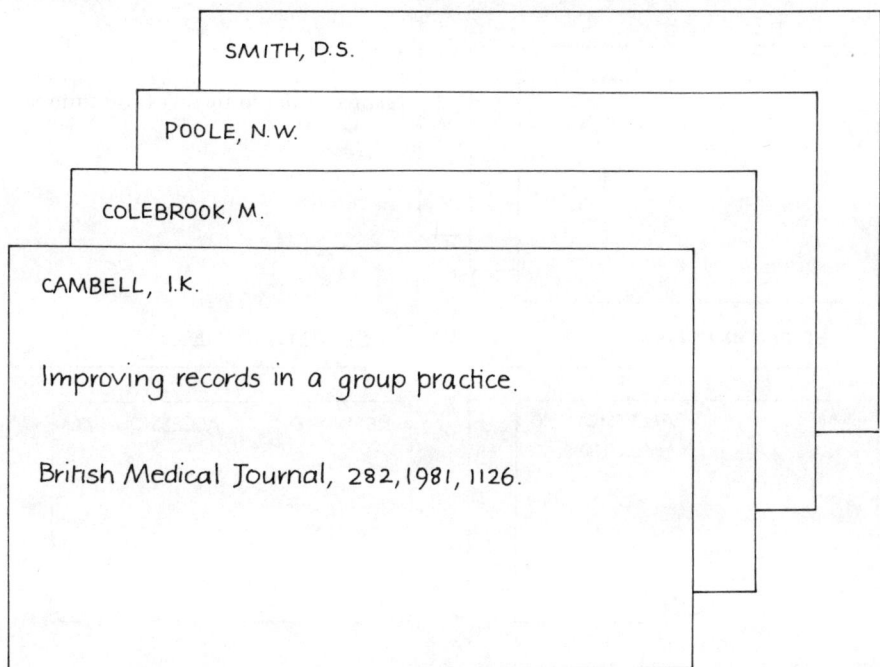

Figure 6.2 Example of a serial system, filed by author

systems. Many unsophisticated computer systems also use this method of storing information. It has the advantage of being simple. However, it has the major disadvantage that access to an individual record is by a single key field (author in the example given above) and access is slow as a serial search through the whole file must be made until the appropriate record is found.

The key field used to organize a serial file will vary depending on the purpose of the file. During the initial stage of a literature search it may be helpful to organize the records according to journal title. This will facilitate the checking of references in a library as the searcher can check all the references for one journal title before moving on to the next title. Once the original articles have been read, it may be helpful to rearrange the file into author or subject order. Within a particular category, it may be helpful to arrange items chronologically with the most recent item filed at the beginning of the sequence. This arrangement enables the person using the file to locate a particular item and if there are a number of items by a particular author or on a particular subject then he will be presented with the most recent item first. In medicine one normally is searching for the most recent information.

Indexed or inverted files

One method of gaining more flexible access to a file is by construcing what is called an indexed or inverted system (*Figure 6.3*). This consists of a series of

132   Medical information: a profile

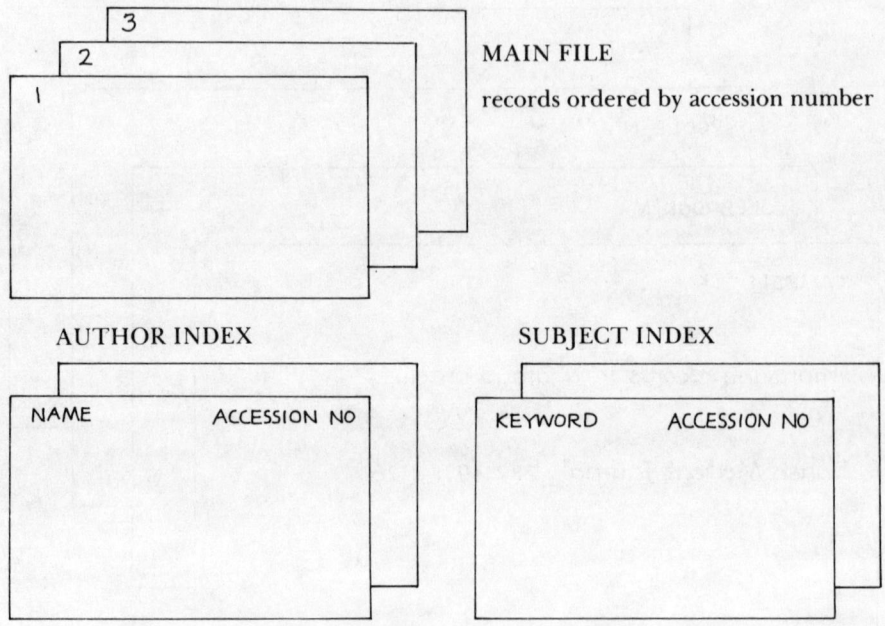

Figure 6.3   Example of an indexed file system

records in either meaningful or random order and a set of indexes. The indexes direct the user to a particular record. There may be a whole series of indexes—for example author, subject, title—each stored in a separate sequence of record cards.

In an indexed file, there is the main sequence of records, i.e. the main file, and a series of indexes to this file. An indexed file may be found in a manual system (although they are quite time-consuming to create and maintain) but more typically in computerized systems. Some of the computer software packages which we shall investigate in more depth later in this chapter are indexed file systems. An indexed file can offer multiple access points to a record and consequently the search process is much faster than in a serial system. The main disadvantage of an indexed file system, however, is that much 'space' is taken up by the additional indexes. In a manual system this extra space implies extra cards, and in a computerized system additional memory capacity.

6.4   Use of microcomputers to organize information

Many people now have access to microcomputers either in their homes or their workplace and they can be used to facilitate the organization and manipulation of large quantities of information. Background information on microcomputers can be readily obtained by reading any of the good introductions to this subject which can be found in most libraries.

This section will be primarily concerned with the different types of software—

that is, computer programs—that can be used to aid the organization of information resources. There are two main types of software packages which are used in this way: database management systems and word processing systems.

Database management systems

Database management systems (DBMS) are software packages that enable information files to be created and used in a flexible manner. These files are normally called databases. DBMS are widely available for most popular microcomputer systems and their cost varies from £15 upwards. Typical examples include dBase II and Inmagic.

DBMS can be used to store a variety of information files from a simple name and address file to a sophisticated drug information file. They are made up of four subsystems, which will be described in turn.

The **data definition language** is the program that enables the user to create the structure of the database. It normally leads the user through a series of questions and his answers determine the structure of the database. The user is normally allowed to give his own name to the file. He must then specify the number of fields in the record. Each field can then be defined in terms of field name, size (if a fixed-field system) and type of data (numeric or alphanumeric). Some data definition languages also enable the user to specify relationships which exist between different data items and also any validation criteria which must be attached to a particular data item, for example that the data in a particular field must be numeric. Sophisticated DBMS enable the system designer to assign access privileges through the provision of a password system and restrict access to particular types of data, individual records or even whole files. Finally, many DBMS provide facilities for changing the structure of a database, for example by adding new fields to a record, something that would normally involve creating a new database structure and writing the data from the old system into the new one.

The **data manipulation language** is the set of programs that enables the user to create records by inputting and editing data, and also to delete records. It can frequently be used to invert or index particular fields in a record. It also enables the user to find a particular record, for example in order that it can be edited.

The size of a simple serial file can be calculated by working out the size of an individual record. In a fixed-field system this is the total number of characters that have been assigned to the record. In a variable-field system we must estimate the average size of a record. The size of a file can then be calculated by multiplying the size of a record by the total number of records. The number obtained will be the number of characters taken up by the computer file. This number is given in bytes, as one character is equivalent to one byte of computer space. Normal practice is to add twenty percent to the size of the file, and also, allowance must be made for growth.

For example, let us calculate the amount of space needed by a serial file:

1 record of fixed field structure takes up 250 characters.
If there are 2,000 records on the file then the size of the file is equal to 500,000 characters.
If the file grows at a rate of 10 percent per annum then the amount of space needed to store the file for 3 years is equal to 500,000 + 150,000 = 650,000 characters.
Allow 20 percent extra space = 780,000 characters
Therefore the total space needed for the file = 780,000 characters, which is approximately equivalent to 780 K bytes, which can be rounded up to 800 K bytes.

This simple calculation enables us to work out the approximate amount of space needed by the file, and shows that the example file can be stored on a disk with a capacity greater than 800 K bytes.

An indexed file requires more space, and there are many algorithms available which enable us to calculate the size of the space required by the file. A rough 'rule of thumb' method which enables us to calculate this space is to work it out as shown above for a serial file and double the answer.

The **query system** is the element of the DBMS which enables the user to access the data in the file; that is, it is the 'user interface'. The query system normally enables the user to:

1. Select an individual record.
2. Carry out searches using Boolean logic.
3. Carry out searches using facilities such as ignoring upper- and lower-case distinctions; truncation searches; and adjacent word searching.
4. Restrict searching to individual fields, groups of fields or the whole record.

Simple DBMS carry out serial searches of the file and are quite slow in operation. More sophisticated systems, which are more expensive, enable indexed or inverted files to be searched. It can be seen from the characteristics of the query system that it has facilities in common with online systems such as DIALOG.

The **reporting system** of a DBMS displays the required information for the user. The display may be on a visual display unit or alternatively on a permanent printout. Users can normally specify the format of their output (e.g. page headings, fields to be printed), order of the items (e.g. sorted by a particular field) and layout within the page or on the screen. Therefore, it is possible for the user to specify the desired output in some detail to suit his own particular needs.

A typical DBMS enables the user to create a number of different files with different parameters. A researcher may require a file of journal references, a name and address file, and also a drug information file. A DBMS package may be used to create these different files each with their own individual record structures.

Two important limitations to using these systems are the memory constraints of the microcomputer and the limitations of the DBMS. The limitations of a DBMS can be found by comparing the following functions for a variety of packages:

What are the record and file limitations?
  Maximum file size
  Maximum record size
  Maximum number of fields
  Maximum number of characters per field
  Types of data—numeric, alphanumeric, logical

How flexible and easy to use are the following functions?
  File creation
  Data input
  Data editing
  Sort facilities
  Search facilities
  Print facilities
  Arithmetic facilities
  Security facilities

How much time (in seconds) does it take to carry out the following processes?
  Add 1 new record
  Sort 50 records
  Search 50 records
  Index 50 records

Word processing software

Word processing software can be used to aid the storage and manipulation of textual data, and is frequently used by information workers to facilitate the storage and presentation of bibliographic information. There is a wide variety of word processing software available for microcomputers, such as the widely used package Wordstar.

Word processing software facilitates all the processes of text input, editing and output, and it can be used to create files of text such as bibliographic references, abstracts, names and addresses, or reports. Word processing packages are frequently used to create and store large quantities of bibliographic information and then to output these as current-awareness bulletins or bibliographies.

Text input

This is achieved by typing in the text and the following facilities aid this process.

  a. End of line determination and wrap-around. This is usually automatic and the typist need not key RETURN at the end of each line. The software identifies the end of each line and moves the text so that left- and right-hand justification is obtained.
  b. Margins. The user can normally set the position of both left- and right-hand margins.
  c. Tabulations. The user can frequently establish a number of tabulation parameters. Some packages include facilities which enable the alignment of decimal points and/or the right-hand side of the columns.

d. Page lengths. The user may be allowed to set the number of lines that will be printed on a page.
e. Page numbering. Some systems have automatic page numbering, others have an option for page numbering, while a few packages do not possess this facility.
f. Headers and footers. Title lines at the top or even the bottom of pages may be inserted automatically throughout a document.

Text editing

Text editing facilities can be used on either a new document or a document file that has been saved (i.e. stored for later use) on the system. The following facilities may be available:

a. Cursor movements. The cursor may be moved left or right a character or word at a time. It may be moved up or down a single line or a group of lines. Moving through a group of lines is called scrolling and it enables the user to move rapidly through the text.
b. Insertions. Single characters, words, sentences, paragraphs or pages may be inserted into the text at a specified place.
c. Deletions. Single characters, words, sentences, paragraphs, pages and whole documents may be deleted.
d. Block movements of text, or 'cut and paste'. Blocks of text may be moved or copied from their present position to another part of the document.
e. Automatic centring. Headings can be automatically placed at the centre of the available line.
f. Sort. Some software packages have a sort facility which enables items to be sorted into alphabetical or numerical order.
g. Find and replace. It is frequently possible to search the text for a specific word or group of words and then to replace automatically them with the desired character set. Options can include: searching the whole or part of a document; searching the text backwards or forwards; ignoring upper- and lower-case distinctions; searching for part or whole words.

Printing

A variety of printing facilities are available and they can be used to enhance the appearance of a document. Examples include:

a. Highlighting. Sections of the text, such as headings, may be typed over twice or three times so that they stand out boldly from the rest of the document.
b. Use of different types of paper. Many printers will accept a variety of paper types, and coloured paper or printed letterheads, for example, can be used to enhance or personalize the final appearance of the document.

Additional facilities

Many word processing packages also possess additional functions which enhance their information processing capabilities.

a. Mailmerge. This important and useful facility enables information from one file, for example one containing names and addresses, to be 'merged' into another file, say one containing a letter, in a specified way.

b. Spelling checks. Some software packages have a facility for checking the spelling in a file. An example of a program which checks spelling is Spellstar. These programs normally have a basic dictionary against which they check all the words in a file. If they come across a word which is not in the dictionary, they will 'ask' the typist if the spelling of that word is correct. If it is then the word will be included in the dictionary, otherwise the spelling of that word can be corrected using the editing facilities.

c. Information retrieval systems. Some word processing systems, such as the Diamond range, possess extremely sophisticated facilities, such as search and sort functions, and they can be used as information retrieval systems. In some cases, it can be difficult to tell whether a package is a word processing or a database management system package.

d. Linking word processing and other software packages. Word processing packages can frequently be linked to other software packages so that information can be processed in an integrated manner. For example, the contents of a file, perhaps one created by a DBMS, can be transferred to a word processing file and then edited for output in a particular way. An example would be as a current-awareness bulletin.

Reference

Stibic, V. *Personal documentation for professionals*. Amsterdam: North-Holland, 1980.

Index

All references are to page numbers. Authors' names are not indexed, nor are book titles except when mentioned in the text.

ABPI Data Sheet Compendium 17–18, 106
abstracting journals 35–45, 93–94
Abstracts of Published Reports 25
accessing a personal record
   system 130–137
Acronyms, initialisms and abbreviations
   dictionary 8
Alcoholics Anonymous 77
American Association for the Study of
   Headache 85
American Book Publishing Record 27
American College of Sports
   Medicine 85
American Dental Association 86
American Journal of Surgery 120
American Medical Association 84
   Journal 30
American medical directory 16, 89
American Ophthalmological Society 85
American Pharmaceutical
   Association 85
AND operator 99–100
Annotated MeSH, *see* MeSH
Antibiotics 92
Aslib Book List 29
Aslib directory of information sources in the
   United Kingdom 12, 78, 87
Aslib Proceedings 59
Australian National Bibliography 27

B-I-T-S, *see* BIOSIS Information Transfer
   System
BIAS, *see* Biomedical Instrumentation
   Advisory Service
bibliographies 26–29
Bibliography of interlingual scientific and
   technical dictionaries 10
Bibliography of scientific, technical and
   specialized dictionaries, a 10

Bibliography of the distribution of disease in
   East Africa 28
BILDSCHIRMTEXT 70
Bioenergy directory 15
Biological Abstracts 39–42, 110, 111, 113,
   116, 118
Biomedical Instrumentation Advisory
   Service 88
BIOSIS 39–42, 49, 60–61, 67, 97, 124
   typical record 51
BIOSIS Information Transfer System 61
BIOSIS Previews 60, 61, 98, 120
BIOSIS Standard Profiles 61
Biotechnology Abstracts 24
Black's medical dictionary 5, 109, 113, 116
BLAISE 97–98
BLLD, *see* British Library Lending
   Division
Blood and its disorders 109
BNF, *see* British National Formulary
Books in Print 27
Boolean logic 99–100
Boots Company plc 87
Brief guide to sources in science and
   technology 113
British Association of Sports
   Medicine 85
British Book News 29
British Books in Print 27
British Dental Association 86
British Library Lending Division 46
British Medical Association 84
British Medical Journal 30
British Medicine: a monthly guide 29, 110,
   111
British Migraine Association 85
British National Bibliography 27, 109
British National Formulary 75, 107, 108
British Optical Association 86

British Reports, Translations and Theses Received by BLLD 25–26, 46, 112
British Union Catalogue of Periodicals 30
BUCOP, *see British Union Catalogue of Periodicals*
Bulletin of the Medical Library Association 59
Bulletin Signalétique 67
Bureau of Medical Practitioner Affairs 70
Butterworths medical dictionary 6, 109, 115

CA Patents 25
CA Search 120, 124
Cancerlit 98, 120
Cancerproj 98
CAPTAIN 71
case studies of searches 105–126
Catalogue of British official publications not published by HMSO 115
CEEFAX 69
Central Patents Index 25
Chemical Abstracts 21, 25, 59, 110, 116
Chemical Reactions Documentation Service 24
CIOMS, *see* Council for International Organizations of Medical Sciences
Citizens Advice Bureau 88
CLAIMS/CHEM 25
CLAIMS/CLASS 25
CLAIMS/US patents 25
CLASS, *see Current Literature Alerting Service* 61
Clinical Notes On-line 61–62
Clinical Research Centre (of the Medical Research Council) 87
Clinproj 98
closed user groups 71
colleagues as sources of information to general practitioners 105
commercial organizations, information departments 87–88
Community Relations Councils 115
computer hardware 53
computer software 55
  for database management 133
  for online searching 57
  for word processing 135
computer terminal, *see* terminal
Consumer health information: a guide to sources 4

Council for International Organizations of Medical Sciences 79
CPI, *see Central Patents Index*
CUGs, *see* closed user groups
Cumulated Index Medicus 37, 93
Current Biotechnology Abstracts 25
Current Contents 44–45, 94, 116, 124
Current Contents: Clinical Practice 44–45, 111, 114, 118
Current Contents: Life Sciences 44–45, 111, 114, 116, 118
Current Literature Alerting Search Service 61
Current Research in Britain 47
Current serials received 30, 31

DAI, *see Dissertation Abstracts International* 47, 95, 111, 113, 117
data retrieval 130–132; *see also* online searching
Data Sheet Compendium, *see ABPI Data Sheet Compendium*
Data-Star 59, 65, 97
data storage 127–130, 132–137
Database 59
database coverage, overlap 124
database management systems 133–135
databooks 16–20
DBMS, *see* database management systems
Decade of viral hepatitis, a 28
Dental-Wörterbuch. Dictionary of dental practice 9
Department of Commerce Library, USA 20
Department of Health and Social Security 83
  Library 88
Derwent Publications Ltd. 24–25, 67
DHSS, *see* Department of Health and Social Security 83
DHSS-DATA 62–63
Dialindex 101–102
DIALOG 57, 59, 97–98, 101, 103
dictionaries 5–10
  language 8–10
  subject 5–8
dictionary file 52
Dictionary of abbreviations in medicine and health sciences 8–9
Dictionary of epidemiology 7–8

Index

directories 11–16
   directories of 11
Directory for exceptional children 15
Directory of agencies serving the visually handicapped in the United States 81, 86
Directory of British associations 12, 78
Directory of directories 11
Directory of European scientific associations 12, 78
Directory of health science libraries in the United States 81, 86
Directory of hospital pharmacists engaged in information work 82
Directory of international and national medical and related societies 12
Directory of international statistics 19
Directory of medical and health care libraries in the United Kingdom and Republic of Ireland 81, 86
DISC, see *Directory of hospital pharmacists engaged in information work* 82
Dissertation Abstracts International 47, 95, 111, 113, 117
document delivery 103
Dorland's illustrated medical dictionary 6
dot matrix printer 54
downloading 59
drug information 106–108
   databooks 17–18
   handbooks 17–18
   on Prestel 74
Drug Information Pharmacists 66
Drug Information Units 82

Electronic Library 59
Elsevier's medical dictionary in five languages 10
EMBASE 63–64, 97–98, 112, 120
EMBASE: Guide to the classification and indexing system 63
EMCLAS: Classification code 64
ESA–IRS 97
Encyclopaedia Britannica 10
Encyclopaedia of antibiotics 92
Encyclopedia of associations 13
Encyclopedia of psychoanalysis 10
encyclopedias 10–11
English–French French–English dictionary of medical and biological terms 9
Euronet 55

Euronet Diane 97
European Patent Convention 24
European Patent Office 21, 24
Excerpta Medica 38–39, 67, 93–94, 97
external sources of information, use by general practitioners 106

Facts about nursing 19
Family Practitioner Service 80
FDC Quality Control 67
Federal library resources, a user's guide to research collections 84
field name 127
field size 127
fields 50, 127
Financial Times index, on teletext 69
FINMED 67
FPS, see Family Practitioner Service
French–English dictionary of physical medicine and rehabilitation 9

General Practitioner 30
general practitioners, sources used by 105–106
glucocorticoid receptors, case study 115–117
government bodies 25, 82–84
Guide to the classification and indexing system (Excerpta Medica) 39, 111
Guide to the documentation of psychology 113
Guide to government departments and other libraries and information bureaux 82
Guide to official statistics 18–19
Guide to reference books (Sheehy) 2, 27, 92, 112
Guide to reference material, see *Walford's Guide to reference material*
Guide to U.S. government statistics 19
Gynecology and Obstetrics 120

handbooks 16–20
Health Libraries Review 59
Health science books 1876–1982 27
Health sciences information sources 3–4, 7, 9, 13, 16, 19, 78
HEEP 124; see also Toxline
Help! I need somebody. A guide to national associations for people in need 13–14, 78, 88
hospital medical libraries 81

host computer 55
host systems, choice of 97–98

Ika, Shika, Waei Hasuon Bunrei Jiten: Japanese–English medical–dental dictionary 10
Illustrated Stedman's medical dictionary 6
Index of Conference Proceedings Received by the BLL 113, 117, 119
Index Medicus 32, 35–39, 65, 93–94, 97
Index to Theses 45–46, 95, 112, 113, 116, 118
indexed files 51, 131–132; *see also* inverted files
indexing journals 35–45, 93–94
Indian Books 27
information providers (for Prestel) 71
Information sources in the history of science and medicine 4–5
Information sources in the medical sciences 2–3, 7, 16, 35, 92, 113, 117
INPI 25
Institute of Medicine 84
Institute of Race Relations 115
International bibliography of special directories 11
International Center of Information on Antibiotics 79
International College of Surgeons 79
International Cystic Fibrosis Association 79
International Journal of Epidemiology 79
International medical who's who 16
International Nursing Abstracts 117
international organizations 78
International Pharmaceutical Abstracts 67, 98, 120, 124
International Union against Tuberculosis 79
inverted files 51, 131–132
IOWA Drug Information Service 107
IPA, see International Pharmaceutical Abstracts 67
Irregular serials and annuals 32, 34

Journal of Dermatology, Surgery and Obstetrics 120
Journal of Information Science 59
Journal of Library Automation 59

Journal of the American Medical Association 30
journals, *see* periodicals

Keyword index to serial titles 31–32
KIST, see Keyword index to serial titles
Kompass 88

Lewis's Quarterly List 28
libraries 80–82, 83–84, 86–88
Library Association. Medical, Health and Welfare Group 81
List of annual reviews on progress in science and technology 32
List of journals abstracted (Excerpta Medica) 38
literature guides 1–5
Lockheed DIALOG 97
log-on procedures in online searching 57

McGraw-Hill encyclopedia of science and technology 11, 106
MALIMET (thesaurus used by *Excerpta Medica*) 38
Man's haemoglobins 109
manual searching 91–95; *see also* the printed sources described in Chapter 1
Martindale: the extra pharmacopoeia 17, 106
Martindale Online 64
 thesaurus 64
MEDIC 67
Medical books and serials in print 28
Medical dictionary: medizinisches Wörterbuch: dictionnaire médical 10
Medical directory 16, 89
Medical Information Research Unit 73, 77, 81
Medical register 16, 89, 110
Medical Research Council 77
Medical research directory 14, 65, 78
Medical research index 14, 78
Medical Subject Headings, *see* MeSH
Medical terminology in hospital practice 8
Medical textbook review 28
'Medicine in the News' 73
Medipage 70, 73
Meditel 73, 74
MEDLARS 35

MEDLARS online, *see Medline*
Medline 65, 97–98, 112, 120, 124
MEDOC 67
mental health and ethnic minorities, case study 112–115
Mental retardation 1971–1980 44; *see also Psychological Abstracts*
MeSH 35–38, 65, 93–94, 98, 110, 112, 118
  tree structures 36
MeSH Supplementary Chemical Record 37
microcomputers
  online searching 58
  searching Prestel 75
  storing information 132–137
MIMS—Monthly Index of Medical Specialities 18, 75, 105, 108
modem 53, 54
Monthly Index of Medical Specialities, see MIMS—Monthly Index of Medical Specialities

National Health Service 77, 79
  library service 80, 81
  professional groups within 80
National Library of Medicine 49
National Library of Medicine Catalog 27
National Library of Medicine Current Catalog 27, 110, 111
National Medical Association 84
New England Journal of Medicine 120
NHS, *see* National Health Service
NLM, *see* National Library of Medicine
Nomenclature and criteria for diagnosis of diseases of the heart and great vessels 9
NOT operator 99–100
nursing libraries 81
Nursing Research Abstracts 119

Official Journal (patents) 24
Oncology Information Service 86
Online 59
Online Information Centre 60
online information retrieval 49–76
online information systems 49–52
Online Review 59
online searching 55–59
  advantages 97
  disadvantages 97

individual databases 34–35, 60–67
printout 101
strategy 98–100
techniques 95–104
of *Ulrich's International periodicals directory* 34–35
OR operator 99–100
OTC: the reference and prescribing aid for pharmacists 108

packet switching 55
Pan-American Medical Association 79
PASCAL 67
Patent Co-operation Treaty 24
patents 20–25
  information network 24
  tracing and locating 21–25
Patents Office, U.K. 21–24
Penguin medical encyclopedia 11
Pergamon–Infoline 97
periodicals 29–35
  guides to 32–35
  tracing 30–32
  use of 30
Permuted MeSH 37
Pestdoc 24
Pharmaceutical handbook 18
Pharmaceutical News Index 67
pharmaceutical representatives 105
Pharmaceutical Society of Great Britain 86
pharmacists, sources used by 108
Pharmline 66
Picture Prestel 72
Prestel, *see* viewdata
Printed reference material 2, 16
printers 54
professional associations 84–86
Program 59
protocol 56
Psychoabs 97, 112
Psychological Abstracts 42–44, 97, 110, 111, 113, 114
Public MeSH, *see* MeSH
PULSE 30

QUEST 97–98
questionnaires 92

RBUPC, see Research in British universities, polytechnics and colleges
recall ratio 120, 123
record cards 91
records 127–130
reference interview 91–92
Regional Drug Information Units, *see* Drug Information Units 82
report literature 25–26
Report of Drug Research 67
representatives as information sources, *see* pharmaceutical representatives
research 47–48
  institutes for 87
Research centers directory: a guide to university-related and other non profit research organizations 87
Research in British universities, polytechnics and colleges 14, 47–48, 78, 89, 111, 116
Ringdoc 21, 24, 25, 67
Roget's thesaurus 9
Roster of federal libraries: agency, geographic, subject 83
Royal College of General Practitioners 85
Royal College of Nursing 86
Royal Society of Medicine 85
RPROJ 67
RTECS 98
Runnymede Trust 115
Russian–English medical dictionary 10

Sage Race Relations Abstracts 115
Science Citation Index 89, 94, 97, 110, 111, 118
Science Reference Library, London 24
Scisearch 97–98
SCONUL, *see* Standing Conference of National and University Libraries
SDC Orbit 97
search failures 125
search strategy 91–104; *see also* manual searching; online searching
search topic definition 91–93
Self-help and the patient: a directory of national organizations concerned with various diseases and handicaps 14–15, 78, 89
sequential file 50

serial file 130–131
serials, *see* periodicals
Serials in the British Library 31, 32
Short English–Swahili medical dictionary, a 10
sickle cell anaemia, case study 109–112
Social Science Citation Index 113, 114
Social Services Abstracts 115
Social Work Information Bulletin 115
social welfare information on Prestel 74
software, *see* computer software
special libraries 59
Standing Conference of National and University Libraries 46–47
statistics, databooks and handbooks 18–20
Statistics and Market Intelligence Library 20
Statistics sources: a subject guide to data on industrial, business, social, educational and financial and other topics for the United States and internationally 19
Stedman's illustrated medical dictionary, see Illustrated Stedman's medical dictionary
stop list 52
storing information 127–130
Surgery 120
Surgical Forum 120

telebanking 72
telecommunications 53, 55
Telenet 55
teleshopping 72
Télésystèmes-Questel 67
teletext 68
  accessing data 68
  costs 69
  information available 69
TELIDON 70
terminal 53
theses 45–47
  availability in the U.K. 46–47
toxicology, information available online 120–126
Toxline 67, 98, 120, 124
Tree structures, *see* MeSH: tree structures
Trent Regional Drug Information Unit 82
Tymnet 55

UKOLUG 60
Ulrich Online 34–35
*Ulrich's International periodicals
  directory* 30, 32–34, 92, 110, 116
Ulrich's Quarterly 34
university medical libraries 80, 86–87

Vetdoc 24
videotex 67–75
viewdata
  costs 75
  definition 70
  development 70
  Gateway 72
  information providers 71
  interaction 71, 72
  international systems 70
  in medicine 72, 73–75
  telebanking 72
  teleshopping 72
  training programmes 74
Virology: an information profile 5
Voluntary Forum Abstracts 115
voluntary organizations 88–89

Walford's Guide to reference material 2, 92
Washington information directory 84
Weekly Pharmacy Reports 67
welfare information on Prestel 74

Welsh Drug Information Unit 82
Wessex Drug Information Service 82
West Midlands Drug Information
  Service 82
WHO, *see* World Health Organization
Wiley Catalog/Online 66
word processing 135–137
*World Book illustrated home medical
  encyclopedia* 24
*World guide to scientific associations and
  learned societies* 84, 86
World Health Organization 77, 78–79
World Intellectual Property
  Organization 24
World list of scientific periodicals 31–32
World Medical Association 79
World of learning 15, 78, 79, 87
World Patent Latest 25
World Patents Abstracts 25
World Patents Index 24
*Wörterbuch der Psychiatrie und medizinischen
  Psychologie* 10
wound healing, effect of infection, case
  study 117–120
WPA, *see World Patents Abstracts*
WPI, *see World Patents Index*

Yearbook of international organizations 15,
  78